Nyla Ashen

Breaking LGBTQ Barriers in Qirona – Unfiltered

Ali Sato

ISBN: 9781779697738
Imprint: Telephasic Workshop
Copyright © 2024 Ali Sato.
All Rights Reserved.

Contents

Introduction   **1**
The Birth of a Trailblazer   1
Embracing Activism   9

Chapter Two   **21**
Section One   21
Section Two   31
Section Three   43

Chapter Three   **55**
Section One   55
Section Two   68
Section Three   78

Conclusion   **91**
The Legacy of Nyla Ashen   91

Index   **101**

Introduction

The Birth of a Trailblazer

Nyla's Unconventional Upbringing

Nyla Ashen, the trailblazing LGBTQ activist, had an upbringing that was anything but conventional. Born into a small town in Qirona, Nyla's childhood was marked by a unique set of circumstances and experiences that shaped her into the fearless advocate she is today.

Growing up in a conservative community, Nyla often felt like she didn't quite fit in. While other children were busy conforming to societal norms, she found solace in questioning those same norms. This curiosity and desire to challenge the status quo were the first signs of her unconventional nature.

Nyla's parents, contrary to the conservative environment they lived in, encouraged her to think freely and express herself openly. They taught her the value of diversity and acceptance, fostering an environment where Nyla's uniqueness was not only celebrated but also encouraged.

One of the most significant influences on Nyla's upbringing was her close relationship with her grandmother. A strong, independent woman, her grandmother challenged traditional gender roles and defied societal expectations. She taught Nyla that she could be whoever she wanted to be, regardless of what others might say.

It was through her grandmother's stories that Nyla discovered the existence of LGBTQ individuals and their struggles. These stories resonated deeply with Nyla, igniting a flame of empathy and compassion within her. She realized that she, too, had a responsibility to fight for the rights and dignity of LGBTQ individuals.

However, Nyla's unconventional upbringing also came with its fair share of challenges. In a community that often rejected anything outside the norm, she experienced prejudice and discrimination from a young age. From being bullied at school to facing judgmental stares from neighbors, Nyla had to learn how to navigate a world that refused to accept her.

But instead of succumbing to the negativity, Nyla found strength in these adversities. She drew inspiration from the LGBTQ activists who came before her, understanding that their struggle was her struggle too. Their courage motivated her to stand up for what she believed in and never back down, regardless of the barriers she faced.

Nyla's unconventional upbringing taught her to question established norms and find her own path. This mindset, combined with her unwavering resilience, laid the foundation for her future as an LGBTQ activist. It was this unique blend of personal experiences, family support, and a burning desire for change that propelled her into the forefront of the LGBTQ rights movement.

By looking beyond the boundaries of her conservative community and embracing her true identity, Nyla Ashen became an inspiration to countless LGBTQ individuals who also felt trapped in the confines of societal expectations. Through her unconventional upbringing, Nyla learned that true strength lies in embracing one's uniqueness and fighting for a more inclusive and accepting world.

As we delve deeper into Nyla's journey, we will witness the profound impact she made on the LGBTQ community, challenging stereotypes, shattering barriers, and breaking new ground in her relentless pursuit of equality and acceptance. Her story will show us that sometimes, it is the most unconventional upbringings that produce the most extraordinary individuals.

Discovering her true identity

Nyla Ashen's journey of self-discovery and embracing her true identity was filled with twists and turns, leading her to become the trailblazing LGBTQ activist she is today. Born and raised in the vibrant city of Qirona, Nyla's unconventional upbringing played a significant role in shaping her understanding of the world and her place in it.

Growing up, Nyla was surrounded by a diverse community that celebrated individuality and encouraged self-expression. Her parents, both artists, instilled in her a deep appreciation for creativity and the freedom to explore different paths. This environment allowed Nyla to embrace her natural curiosity and question societal norms from an early age.

As Nyla reached adolescence, she began to realize that her assigned gender did not align with her innermost feelings. This realization marked the beginning of her journey towards self-discovery. Despite societal expectations and the fear of judgment, Nyla mustered the courage to explore her identity, seeking solace in the LGBTQ community.

Her first encounter with the LGBTQ community came through online forums and support groups where she connected with individuals who had similar experiences. These virtual spaces provided a safe haven for Nyla to explore her true identity and gain a deeper understanding of herself. Through heartfelt conversations with members of the LGBTQ community, Nyla discovered that she was not alone in her journey and that there was strength in embracing one's authentic self.

Inspired by the stories of LGBTQ role models who had triumphed over adversity, Nyla embarked on a mission to understand herself better. She devoured memoirs and autobiographies of LGBTQ individuals, finding solace and inspiration in their shared experiences. These stories became a powerful catalyst for Nyla's self-acceptance and understanding, as they illuminated the path towards her true identity.

Navigating the road to self-discovery was not easy for Nyla. She faced numerous hurdles, including moments of self-doubt and societal pressures. However, each challenge she encountered only fueled her determination to break free from the constraints of societal norms and embrace her true self.

Nyla's journey of self-discovery was not without its unique moments of realization. In a world where gender norms are often rigidly defined, Nyla found herself questioning the binary understanding of gender. Through extensive research and deep introspection, she came to understand the fluidity of gender and the vast spectrum of identities that exist beyond the traditional binaries.

In her quest to discover her true identity, Nyla explored various aspects of her personality, embracing the intersectionality of her experiences. She delved into the realm of intersectional feminism, where she discovered the importance of acknowledging the interconnectedness of different forms of oppression. This realization not only helped Nyla understand herself better but also provided her with a broader perspective on activism and the need for inclusivity in all aspects of society.

In this section, we delved into Nyla Ashen's personal journey of self-discovery and the pivotal moments that led her to embrace her true identity. From her unconventional upbringing to the influence of LGBTQ role models, Nyla's path towards self-acceptance was filled with challenges and triumphs. Her journey serves as an inspiration to countless individuals who are navigating their own paths, offering hope and validation to those who are on a similar quest of self-discovery and acceptance.

The influence of her LGBTQ role models

Nyla Ashen's journey towards discovering her true identity and embracing her role as a LGBTQ activist was shaped significantly by the presence of influential role models in her life. These role models served as guiding lights, providing Nyla with inspiration, support, and a sense of belonging. In this section, we will explore the profound impact they had on Nyla's personal and professional development.

Throughout her unconventional upbringing, Nyla was exposed to a diverse range of LGBTQ individuals who challenged societal norms and dared to live authentically. From her early years, Nyla found solace in their stories and experiences, recognizing the strength and resilience it took to navigate a world that often rejected them. These role models became her source of inspiration, giving her the courage to confront her own identity and embrace her truth.

One of Nyla's LGBTQ role models was Alex Diaz, a prominent LGBTQ activist and artist. Alex's unapologetic attitude and unwavering dedication to advocacy deeply resonated with Nyla. She admired his ability to use his platform to elevate the voices of the marginalized and his unwavering commitment to creating a more inclusive society. Alex's artistic expressions became a source of inspiration for Nyla, motivating her to explore her own creativity as a means of advocating for change.

Another influential figure in Nyla's life was Sarah Anderson, a transgender rights activist. Sarah's unwavering determination and ability to navigate complex legal battles in her fight for transgender rights deeply impacted Nyla. She admired Sarah's resilience in the face of adversity and her ability to bring about tangible change through her legal victories. Sarah's activism inspired Nyla to pursue a career in law, recognizing the transformative power of challenging discriminatory policies and laws.

Nyla's role models extended beyond those within her immediate community. She found support and inspiration from LGBTQ activists across the globe, whose stories resonated with her own experiences. One such role model was Zara Ahmed, an LGBTQ rights advocate from Pakistan. Zara's fearless activism in a country with deeply ingrained societal prejudices spoke volumes to Nyla. She recognized the importance of intersectionality in the fight for LGBTQ rights and was inspired by Zara's courage to challenge cultural norms.

Nyla's role models taught her valuable lessons about resilience, authenticity, and the power of community. They instilled in her the belief that change starts with individual bravery and the unyielding pursuit of equality and acceptance. Their stories served as a reminder that progress is possible, even in the face of overwhelming opposition.

Nyla's relationship with her role models was not limited to admiration alone. She sought mentorship and guidance from them, which played a crucial role in shaping her journey as an LGBTQ activist. They provided insight, shared their experiences, and helped her navigate the complex landscape of advocacy. This mentorship relationship enabled Nyla to avoid common pitfalls, learn from their successes and failures, and develop her own unique approach to activism.

In addition to her LGBTQ role models, Nyla also found support and inspiration within her own community. The LGBTQ organizations in Qirona, where Nyla actively participated, became an invaluable resource for her. They provided a safe space for her to connect with individuals who shared similar struggles and aspirations. The camaraderie and shared experiences within these organizations motivated Nyla to continue her activism and fueled her determination to create lasting change.

The influence of Nyla's LGBTQ role models extended far beyond her personal life. They laid the foundation for her successful career as an activist and provided a roadmap for challenging discriminatory laws and policies. By standing on the shoulders of giants, Nyla was able to pave her own path while building upon the legacy of those who came before her.

It is worth noting that finding LGBTQ role models and seeking their guidance is not limited to just LGBTQ individuals. Allies also have a crucial role to play in creating an inclusive society. By demonstrating support, empathy, and a willingness to learn, allies can become powerful advocates in the fight for LGBTQ rights. Nyla's own journey highlighted the vital role allies played in her fight against discrimination.

In conclusion, the influence of LGBTQ role models on Nyla Ashen's journey cannot be overstated. Their stories, experiences, and mentorship were instrumental in shaping her identity as an activist and provided her with a strong foundation to fight for equality and acceptance. Through their inspiration, Nyla learned the importance of resilience, authenticity, and the power of community in effecting change. Their legacy lives on in Nyla's work, empowering future generations to continue the fight for LGBTQ rights.

Nyla's Early Encounters with Discrimination

Nyla Ashen, a true trailblazer in the LGBTQ community, faced early encounters with discrimination that shaped her journey as an activist. Growing up in a small town in Qirona, Nyla's unconventional upbringing exposed her to the harsh realities of prejudice and intolerance.

As a young child, Nyla didn't fit into the traditional gender norms imposed by society. While her peers happily played with toys of their assigned gender, Nyla found solace in exploring her true identity. However, these innocent expressions of self-discovery were met with confusion and disapproval from those around her.

Nyla's parents, recognizing her unique spirit, stood by her side and provided the love and support she needed during these challenging times. However, the outside world was not as accepting. Nyla often faced ridicule and discrimination from classmates and teachers who didn't understand her non-binary identity.

These early encounters with discrimination had a profound impact on Nyla. Determined to rise above the hate, she channeled her pain into a drive for change. Nyla found inspiration in LGBTQ role models who bravely fought against injustice, sparking her determination to make a difference.

Nyla's teenage years were marked by further instances of discrimination. Bullied for her authentic expression, Nyla became acutely aware of the bigotry that ran deep within society. Rather than allowing it to break her spirit, Nyla used these experiences as fuel for her activism.

She learned to find strength in adversity, forging ahead and committing herself to creating a more inclusive and accepting world. Nyla's early encounters with discrimination taught her the power of resilience and the importance of standing up for oneself, serving as the foundation for her future activism.

It was through the adversity she faced that Nyla discovered her unwavering passion for standing up for LGBTQ rights. These challenging moments ignited her determination to fight for equality, not only for herself but for countless others who faced similar discrimination.

Nyla's early encounters with discrimination were not a hindrance but a catalyst for her transformation into a powerful advocate for change. She knew that by sharing her story and fighting against injustice, she could break down the barriers that prevented LGBTQ individuals from fully embracing their identities.

As Nyla's activism would soon show, her early encounters with discrimination sparked a fire within her that would continue to burn brightly throughout her remarkable journey. With unyielding determination and a fierce resolve, Nyla would become a beacon of hope for the LGBTQ community, proving that love and acceptance can triumph over hate and discrimination.

Finding Strength in Adversity

In the face of discrimination and hardship, Nyla Ashen discovered her inner strength and resilience, becoming an unwavering force in the LGBTQ community. Her journey is a testament to the power of determination and the refusal to let adversity define one's identity.

Overcoming Challenges

Throughout her life, Nyla faced numerous challenges that tested her resolve. From a young age, she encountered prejudice and ignorance directed towards her LGBTQ identity. She endured hurtful slurs, judgmental glances, and even physical harm. Instead of allowing these experiences to break her spirit, Nyla found strength in the midst of adversity.

One of the key ways Nyla tackled discrimination was by educating herself and others. She delved into the history of LGBTQ rights movements, studied the legal aspects of discrimination, and thoroughly understood the hardships faced by LGBTQ individuals around the world.

Equipped with this knowledge, Nyla actively engaged in conversations with those who held prejudiced views. She showed empathy and compassion, patiently debunking misconceptions and challenging negative stereotypes. By sharing her own personal story and experiences, Nyla humanized the struggles faced by LGBTQ individuals, fostering understanding and fostering dialogue.

Building a Support Network

In her journey towards self-acceptance, Nyla recognized the importance of surrounding herself with a supportive network of friends, family, and mentors who understood her true identity. She sought solace in LGBTQ support groups, finding individuals who had walked a similar path and could provide guidance and encouragement.

These connections not only offered emotional support but also provided practical advice on navigating discriminatory environments. Nyla learned various strategies to assert her rights, including documenting instances of discrimination, seeking legal recourse, and collaborating with other activists to initiate change.

Furthermore, Nyla believed in the power of building alliances beyond the LGBTQ community. She actively sought out individuals and organizations who shared her vision for equality and acceptance. By forging partnerships with allies, regardless of their sexual orientation or gender identity, Nyla expanded her sphere of influence, amplifying her voice and reaching a broader audience.

Turning Adversity into Motivation

Rather than allowing discrimination to discourage her, Nyla transformed her experiences into fuel for her activism. She channeled her frustrations and anger into positive action, working tirelessly to dismantle discriminatory systems and create a more inclusive society.

Nyla recognized the importance of resilience in the face of adversity. She often spoke about the need for mental strength and self-care in order to sustain the fight for LGBTQ rights. Through mindfulness practices, exercise, and seeking support from loved ones, Nyla ensured her own well-being while advocating for others.

Moreover, Nyla harnessed the power of storytelling to inspire and uplift those facing similar challenges. She shared her journey openly, highlighting both the triumphs and struggles she encountered along the way. By providing a voice to those who felt marginalized, Nyla instilled hope and resilience in others, empowering them to embrace their true selves.

Unconventional Strategies

In her pursuit of LGBTQ equality, Nyla approached advocacy with a sense of creativity and innovation. She understood that traditional methods alone weren't always effective in breaking down barriers, so she employed unconventional strategies to make a lasting impact.

One such strategy involved leveraging humor and wit to disarm opposition and engage wider audiences. Through clever satire and playful commentary, Nyla challenged deeply rooted prejudices, encouraging people to question their own biases in a non-threatening manner.

Nyla also recognized the potential of using art and culture as vehicles for change. She collaborated with LGBTQ artists, musicians, and writers to create powerful works that celebrated diversity and promoted acceptance. These collaborations helped foster conversations, spark empathy, and challenge societal norms.

Celebrating Personal Growth

Nyla's journey was not just about activism but also about personal growth and self-discovery. Along the way, she embraced her own identity, navigating the complexities of love, relationships, and self-acceptance. Through her experiences, she developed resilience, compassion, and a deep understanding of the human spirit.

Nyla's ability to find strength in adversity serves as an inspiration to all. Her unwavering determination, combined with her unique approach to advocacy, propelled her to the forefront of the LGBTQ rights movement. Nyla Ashen is a true trailblazer, leaving a legacy of acceptance, equality, and hope for future generations.

Exercise: Reflect on a time when you faced adversity and identify the strengths you developed as a result. How can you use these strengths to inspire and empower others?

Embracing Activism

Nyla's journey to becoming an activist

Nyla Ashen's transformation from a young individual navigating her own identity to a fearless LGBTQ activist is a captivating tale filled with self-discovery, resilience, and a passion for advocating for change. Her journey unfolds against the backdrop of Qirona, a society grappling with deep-rooted prejudices and discriminatory practices.

Born into an unconventional upbringing, Nyla's childhood was marked by curiosity and a drive to question societal norms. Growing up in a small town, she was exposed to limited perspectives on gender and sexuality. However, Nyla's strong sense of self and unwavering determination propelled her towards a path of self-discovery.

Throughout her teenage years, Nyla grappled with her true identity. She found solace and inspiration through the stories of LGBTQ individuals who had fought to assert their rights and live authentically. These LGBTQ role models became a guiding light for Nyla during her formative years, showing her that it was possible to carve out a space for herself and make a meaningful impact.

Nyla's early encounters with discrimination, both subtle and overt, fueled her desire to effect change. Instances of prejudice, whether it was facing derogatory slurs or witnessing the exclusion of LGBTQ individuals, propelled Nyla into action. Instead of allowing these experiences to weaken her spirit, she found strength in adversity, vowing to challenge societal norms and foster a more inclusive world.

Embracing activism became a natural progression for Nyla. Driven by a deep sense of empathy and a passion for justice, she embarked on a journey to make a difference in the lives of LGBTQ individuals. Nyla sought out LGBTQ organizations in Qirona, finding like-minded individuals who shared her vision for change.

Nyla's journey towards becoming an activist was not without its challenges. The impact of her activism on her personal life was significant; she faced backlash from some family members and friends who struggled to accept her new path. However, Nyla's unwavering commitment to the cause propelled her forward, reminding her of the importance of fighting for equality and acceptance.

What set Nyla apart was her unique approach to advocacy. Rather than solely relying on anger and confrontation, she employed humor and wit as powerful tools to engage others in critical conversations. Nyla recognized that making a meaningful impact required reaching hearts and minds, and she used her charming personality and quick wit to disarm opposition and bridge divides.

Nyla's rise to prominence in the LGBTQ community came as no surprise. Her authentic voice and engaging style resonated with people from all walks of life. She built a reputation for fearlessly speaking truth to power, challenging discriminatory practices, and championing the rights of LGBTQ individuals.

Through her groundbreaking LGBTQ campaign, Nyla dared to disrupt the status quo, igniting conversations and challenging deep-rooted prejudices. Despite facing opposition and backlash, she persevered, fueled by the power of allies who rallied behind her cause. Nyla understood that true change required solidarity and unity, and she fostered collaborations with individuals and organizations passionate about dismantling discriminatory systems.

The impact of media on Nyla's activism cannot be underestimated. She harnessed the power of various platforms, using TV interviews and talk shows to amplify her message of inclusivity and educate the broader public. Nyla's viral social media moments further propelled her into the spotlight, showing the world the strength and resilience of the LGBTQ community.

Nyla recognized the immense importance of representation in the media and worked tirelessly to showcase diverse voices and narratives. Collaborating with LGBTQ influencers, she harnessed the power of social media to broaden the conversation around LGBTQ rights and foster a sense of community.

Her alliance with LGBTQ celebrities not only elevated her cause but also brought much-needed attention and advocacy to Qirona's LGBTQ community. Nyla understood the significance of LGBTQ representation in the entertainment industry, leveraging her connections to push for more inclusive storytelling.

However, with fame comes rumors and controversies. Nyla's personal life often fell under intense scrutiny, and rumors about her relationships regularly made headlines. Instead of shying away from the spotlight, Nyla used these moments to create meaningful dialogues, challenging societal norms around love, relationships, and sexuality.

Nyla's influence extended beyond media appearances and viral moments; she found a powerful platform through inspirational speeches and TED talks. Her ability to captivate audiences with her eloquence and authenticity made her a sought-after speaker at LGBTQ conferences worldwide. Nyla's words resonated deeply with LGBTQ youth around the world, inspiring them to embrace their true selves and challenging them to fight for a more equal and accepting future.

Nyla's journey to becoming an activist was not without personal struggles. Navigating relationships and love as an LGBTQ activist presented its own unique set of challenges, as she constantly negotiated her public and private identities. Coming out to her family and community was a defining moment in her life, showcasing her bravery and resilience.

Mental health and self-care became essential components of Nyla's life as an activist. She recognized the toll that constant advocacy could take on her well-being and made it a priority to address her own needs. Nyla openly discussed the importance of mental health and self-care, challenging the notion that activists should sacrifice their well-being for the cause.

Finding balance between activism and personal life was an ongoing journey for Nyla. She understood that taking care of herself was crucial for sustaining her fight for equality and acceptance. Nyla's journey serves as a reminder of the complex, multifaceted nature of activism and the importance of maintaining a strong sense of self amidst the challenges of fighting for change.

Nyla Ashen's journey to becoming an activist is a testament to the transformative power of embracing one's true identity and using it as a catalyst for change. Her legacy continues to shape LGBTQ rights in Qirona, inspiring future generations to stand up, speak out, and break down barriers. As the world celebrates her trailblazing journey, Nyla's words of inspiration echo: "You are not alone. Your voice matters. Together, we can create a world where everyone is free to be their authentic selves."

By recounting Nyla Ashen's journey, we hope to celebrate her accomplishments, inspire future activists, and foster a world that embraces and celebrates the diversity of the LGBTQ community.

Joining LGBTQ organizations in Qirona

Nyla's decision to become an activist was not taken lightly. After coming to terms with her own identity, she felt a burning desire to fight for the rights and acceptance of the LGBTQ community in her hometown of Qirona. In order to be effective in her mission, Nyla knew she needed to connect with like-minded individuals and organizations. This led her on a journey of joining LGBTQ organizations in Qirona, where she would find a sense of belonging and a platform to drive real change.

The Importance of LGBTQ Organizations

LGBTQ organizations play a crucial role in advocating for the rights and well-being of the LGBTQ community. These organizations provide support, resources, and a sense of community for individuals who identify as LGBTQ, as well as their allies. By joining such organizations, Nyla saw an opportunity to not only contribute to the cause but also to learn from the experiences of others who have fought similar battles.

One of the first organizations Nyla joined was "Rainbow Rising," a grassroots LGBTQ rights group that focused on education, awareness, and community engagement. Through her involvement with Rainbow Rising, Nyla attended workshops, seminars, and events that fostered inclusivity and challenged discriminatory practices in Qirona. She found solace in the diverse group of individuals who shared their personal stories, struggles, and triumphs. These shared experiences created a bond that transcended societal barriers.

Building Connections

In addition to Rainbow Rising, Nyla also sought out other LGBTQ organizations in Qirona to broaden her network and impact. She connected with "Equal Hearts," an organization that provided support and resources for LGBTQ youth in the city. By volunteering her time and skills, Nyla became a mentor to young individuals, offering guidance and support during their journey of self-discovery.

By actively participating in LGBTQ organizations, Nyla was able to establish meaningful connections with individuals who shared her passion for equality and acceptance. These connections proved to be invaluable as they served as a support system, offering advice, guidance, and collective strength during difficult times. In turn, Nyla reciprocated this support by sharing her own experiences and lending a listening ear to those who needed it.

Collaborative Advocacy

Joining LGBTQ organizations not only allowed Nyla to connect with individuals, but it also opened doors for collaborative advocacy efforts. Nyla realized that by working together with like-minded organizations, they could amplify their message, garner public attention, and drive change more effectively.

Through partnerships with organizations such as "Pride Alliance" and "Queer Rights Collective," Nyla participated in marches, rallies, and awareness campaigns that challenged societal prejudices and discriminatory laws. These united efforts sent a powerful message to the public and policymakers, demanding equal rights and opportunities for all individuals, regardless of their sexual orientation or gender identity.

Embracing Unconventional Approaches

As Nyla became more involved in LGBTQ organizations, she recognized the need for innovative and unconventional approaches to advocacy. She believed that laughter, creativity, and storytelling could break down barriers and challenge societal norms more effectively than anger or confrontation.

With this mindset, Nyla collaborated with a local LGBTQ theater group called "Broadway Beyond Boundaries." Together, they created thought-provoking and entertaining performances that tackled LGBTQ issues with wit, humor, and empathy. These performances not only entertained audiences but also sparked conversations and encouraged critical thinking, ultimately promoting greater understanding and acceptance.

Outreach Programs for Education and Acceptance

In her journey of joining LGBTQ organizations, Nyla realized the importance of providing education and promoting acceptance at all levels of society. She actively participated in outreach programs organized by LGBTQ organizations, visiting schools, colleges, and community centers to deliver workshops and presentations on LGBTQ history, rights, and challenges.

These programs aimed to dispel myths, address misconceptions, and foster inclusive environments. Nyla shared her personal journey and experiences, providing a relatable perspective that encouraged empathy and understanding. By working directly with educators and community leaders, Nyla helped shape LGBTQ-inclusive curricula, policies, and support systems that benefited countless individuals in Qirona.

Thinking beyond Qirona

Nyla's involvement with LGBTQ organizations in Qirona not only made a significant impact locally but also allowed her to envision a larger goal - the global fight for LGBTQ rights. Through networking and collaborative efforts, Nyla connected with activists from different parts of the world, learning about their struggles and strategies.

This global perspective strengthened Nyla's resolve to continue her activism, realizing that the fight for LGBTQ rights transcended geographical boundaries. She shared her own experiences and the lessons learned from LGBTQ organizations in Qirona, aiming to inspire others to join the cause and work towards a more inclusive and accepting world.

Breaking Barriers, Building Bridges

Joining LGBTQ organizations in Qirona proved to be an integral part of Nyla's journey as an activist. Through these organizations, she found solidarity, support, and a sense of purpose. By connecting with individuals and collaborating with like-minded organizations, Nyla expanded her influence and made a tangible difference in promoting LGBTQ rights and acceptance.

Nyla's experience with LGBTQ organizations taught her the power of community, advocacy, and unconventional approaches. It was through these connections and collective efforts that she was able to break down barriers, challenge societal norms, and build bridges towards a more inclusive and accepting future. The next chapter of Nyla's journey would take her on a groundbreaking LGBTQ campaign that would leave an indelible mark on Qirona and beyond.

The impact of Nyla's activism on her personal life

Nyla's journey into activism brought about significant changes in her personal life. As she began to immerse herself in the LGBTQ community and fight for equality and acceptance, her relationships, self-perception, and daily routines were all affected.

First and foremost, Nyla's activism helped her discover her true self and find a sense of belonging. Through her work with LGBTQ organizations in Qirona, she connected with others who shared similar experiences, struggles, and aspirations. This sense of community gave her the strength and support she needed to embrace her identity fully.

However, Nyla's newfound activism also presented its fair share of challenges in her personal relationships. Her dedication to advocacy often demanded long hours, leaving little time for friends and family. This led to strained relationships and a need to reassess her priorities. Nyla had to strike a delicate balance between her passion for activism and her personal connections.

Moreover, her activism brought her into the limelight, making her a public figure. This sudden fame put a spotlight on her personal life, resulting in invasive media attention and public scrutiny. Nyla had to navigate the delicate balance between maintaining her privacy and using her platform to raise awareness and create change. This constant pressure challenged her emotional well-being, forcing her to develop strategies for self-care and mental resilience.

Nyla's activism also influenced her career choices and educational pursuits. Her commitment to creating a more inclusive society pushed her to explore opportunities in law and policy-making. She saw these fields as avenues for effecting lasting change and breaking down discriminatory barriers. Nyla's activism shaped her academic and professional trajectory, guiding her towards channels that aligned with her values and aspirations.

In terms of personal growth, Nyla's activism provided her with a sense of purpose and fulfillment. She experienced the exhilarating highs of victories, such as successful campaigns or groundbreaking court cases, but also faced the disappointments and setbacks inherent in any activist's journey. However, these challenges only fueled her determination and resilience.

Beyond the direct impact on her personal life, Nyla's activism also had a profound effect on her self-esteem and self-worth. Through her efforts, she discovered her own strength, courage, and ability to create change. Nyla became an inspiration not only to others but also to herself.

In conclusion, the impact of Nyla's activism on her personal life was multi-faceted. It brought about self-discovery, personal growth, and a sense of belonging. It also introduced various challenges, such as strained relationships and media scrutiny. However, through it all, Nyla's dedication to advocacy empowered her, allowing her to not only make significant contributions to the LGBTQ movement but also find fulfillment and purpose in her own life.

Nyla's Unique Approach to Advocacy

Nyla Ashen's journey as an LGBTQ activist is not only defined by her tireless advocacy, but also by her unique approach to spreading awareness and fighting for equality. Standing at the forefront of the LGBTQ rights movement in Qirona, Nyla has earned a reputation for her innovative strategies and unconventional methods. In this section, we will explore some of the key aspects that define Nyla's distinctive approach to advocacy.

Authenticity: The Power of Personal Storytelling

One of the most notable aspects of Nyla's advocacy is her unwavering commitment to authenticity. She understands the power of personal storytelling in conveying the human experience and creating empathy in others. Nyla has been unafraid to share her own struggles and triumphs, offering a heartfelt and relatable narrative that resonates with people from different walks of life.

By openly discussing her journey of self-discovery and acceptance, Nyla invites others to embrace their own identities and challenges societal norms. Through her vulnerability, she empowers individuals to embrace their authentic selves and recognize the value of diversity within the LGBTQ community.

Inclusive Collaboration: Amplifying Voices

Nyla firmly believes in the strength of unity and inclusivity. She recognizes that advocating for LGBTQ rights requires the collective efforts of diverse individuals and communities. In her advocacy work, Nyla actively seeks out collaborations with individuals from various backgrounds, including different sexual orientations, gender identities, ethnicities, and socioeconomic statuses.

By amplifying the voices of marginalized groups within the LGBTQ community, Nyla ensures that their unique challenges and experiences are heard and validated. Through inclusive collaborations, she fosters a sense of belonging and empowers individuals to be active participants in the fight for equality.

Creative Activism: Breaking Down Barriers

Nyla's approach to activism is characterized by her creativity and a willingness to think outside the box. She understands that traditional methods of advocacy may not always be effective in breaking down societal barriers and challenging heteronormative norms. As such, she embraces unconventional approaches that are attention-grabbing and thought-provoking.

From organizing flash mobs and street performances to collaborating with artists to create LGBTQ-themed art installations, Nyla ensures that her activism is visible and impactful. By creating moments that demand attention and spark conversation, she breaks down stigmas and encourages open dialogue about LGBTQ issues.

Humor as a Tool: Disarming Stereotypes

An element that sets Nyla apart is her clever use of humor to address misconceptions and stereotypes surrounding the LGBTQ community. She recognizes that humor can be a powerful tool for disarming prejudices and fostering understanding. Through witty speeches, satirical performances, and humorous social media content, Nyla challenges societal norms with a lighthearted approach.

By using humor, Nyla engages both LGBTQ individuals and allies, creating a space for conversations that might otherwise be uncomfortable. Through comedy, she invites individuals to examine their own biases and encourages them to question societal standards.

Empowering the Next Generation: Education and Mentorship

Nyla understands the importance of education and mentorship in creating lasting change. She actively engages with LGBTQ youth, providing support and guidance through mentorship programs and collaborations with educational institutions. By sharing her experiences and knowledge, Nyla empowers the next generation of LGBTQ activists to continue the fight for equality.

Through workshops, panel discussions, and educational campaigns, Nyla helps educate both young people and the broader community about LGBTQ rights and issues. By prioritizing education and mentorship, she ensures the sustainability and growth of the LGBTQ rights movement in Qirona.

In conclusion, Nyla Ashen's unique approach to advocacy has made a profound impact on the LGBTQ rights movement in Qirona. Through authenticity, inclusive collaboration, creative activism, the use of humor, and empowering the next generation, she has helped pave the way for greater acceptance and equality. Nyla's unwavering dedication to breaking barriers and challenging societal norms continues to inspire countless individuals and brings hope for a more inclusive and equitable future for all.

Making a name for herself in the LGBTQ community

Nyla Ashen's journey towards becoming a prominent figure in the LGBTQ community was not an easy one. She faced numerous challenges and obstacles, but her determination and unwavering passion for equality helped her carve a path for herself.

Navigating LGBTQ Spaces

At the beginning of her activism, Nyla faced the challenge of finding her place within LGBTQ spaces. While she was embraced by some, others questioned her credibility and commitment to the cause. Nyla understood the importance of gaining respect and recognition within the LGBTQ community, and she approached this task with grace and humility.

To build trust and establish herself as a respected advocate, Nyla actively engaged with local LGBTQ organizations in Qirona. She attended community events, participated in panel discussions, and volunteered her time and skills to support various initiatives. By immersing herself in the community, Nyla learned from the experiences and perspectives of other activists, which further shaped her understanding of the diverse challenges faced by LGBTQ individuals in Qirona.

Amplifying Voices

One of the key ways Nyla made a name for herself was by amplifying the voices of marginalized members of the LGBTQ community. She recognized that many individuals had valuable stories and perspectives that were often overlooked or ignored.

Nyla started a series of interviews and podcasts called "Untold Stories," where she provided a platform for LGBTQ individuals to share their experiences and struggles. These stories ranged from deeply personal tales of coming out to inspiring narratives of resilience and triumph. Through this initiative, Nyla sought to create empathy and understanding among the broader public and highlight the rich diversity within the LGBTQ community.

Collaborative Partnerships

Nyla believed in the power of unity and collaboration. She actively sought out partnerships with other LGBTQ activists, organizations, and influencers. By joining forces, they could amplify their messages, pool resources, and create a stronger impact.

Through collaborations with well-established LGBTQ organizations, Nyla gained access to larger platforms and resources that helped elevate her message. She also collaborated with influencers from various fields, such as music, art, and fashion, to bridge the gap between the LGBTQ community and mainstream culture. These partnerships allowed Nyla to reach a broader audience and break down barriers within society.

Challenging Stereotypes

Another way Nyla made a name for herself was by challenging stereotypes associated with LGBTQ individuals. She defied expectations and broke down barriers through her unique approach to advocacy.

Nyla leveraged her background in stand-up comedy to inject humor and wit into her activism. She used satire and clever wordplay to shed light on serious issues while also challenging societal norms and biases. Her unconventional style not only generated attention but also helped change the narrative surrounding LGBTQ individuals. Through her comedic activism, Nyla showed the world that activism doesn't have to be serious and somber, but can also be vibrant, inclusive, and entertaining.

Educational Initiatives

Recognizing the need for education and awareness, Nyla launched several initiatives to promote LGBTQ inclusivity and acceptance. She worked closely with schools, colleges, and educational institutions to implement LGBTQ-inclusive curricula and provide training to teachers and faculty.

Nyla's educational initiatives also targeted the general public. She conducted workshops and seminars on LGBTQ history, rights, and issues, aiming to dispel misconceptions and foster empathy. These efforts played a crucial role in breaking down barriers, promoting understanding, and cultivating a more inclusive society.

In conclusion, Nyla Ashen's journey to making a name for herself in the LGBTQ community was driven by her determination, authenticity, and commitment to equality. Through her active engagement in LGBTQ spaces, amplification of marginalized voices, collaborative partnerships, challenge of stereotypes, and educational initiatives, she carved a unique space for herself as a trailblazing advocate. Nyla's unconventional yet effective approach helped her resonate with a broad audience, paving the way for a more inclusive and accepting society.

Chapter Two

Section One

Nyla's Groundbreaking LGBTQ Campaign

Nyla Ashen's groundbreaking LGBTQ campaign in Qirona was a catalyst for change, pushing the boundaries of acceptance and creating a more inclusive society. This section explores the key elements of Nyla's campaign, from its inception to its remarkable impact.

The Need for Change

Nyla recognized the pressing need for change in Qirona's LGBTQ rights landscape. Discrimination and prejudice against the LGBTQ community were deeply ingrained in society, impacting individuals' lives and limiting their opportunities. Nyla's campaign aimed to challenge these barriers and foster a society that celebrates diversity.

Raising Awareness

An essential aspect of Nyla's campaign was raising awareness about LGBTQ issues and the importance of equality. She organized public events, partnered with LGBTQ organizations, and engaged with community members to educate them about the challenges faced by the LGBTQ community. Nyla's infectious enthusiasm and knack for storytelling helped her connect with people on a personal level, sparking empathy and understanding.

Empowering LGBTQ Youth

Nyla's campaign placed a strong emphasis on empowering LGBTQ youth. She recognized that they were particularly vulnerable to discrimination and lacked adequate support systems. Nyla established mentorship programs, safe spaces, and counseling services to provide a nurturing environment for LGBTQ youth. She also organized workshops and seminars to equip them with essential life skills and empower them to become advocates for change.

Collaboration and Allyship

Nyla understood the power of collaboration and allyship in effecting change. She actively sought partnerships with organizations from various backgrounds, including faith-based groups, educational institutions, and businesses. Nyla encouraged open dialogue, bridging the gap between different communities and fostering understanding. Her campaign successfully created a broad coalition of allies who stood together in support of LGBTQ rights.

Creative and Inclusive Campaign Strategies

Nyla's campaign strategies were known for their creativity and inclusivity. She leveraged various media platforms, such as social media, television, and print, to amplify her message and engage a wide audience. Nyla's team developed visually appealing infographics, relatable memes, and powerful storytelling techniques to make LGBTQ issues accessible and relatable to people from all walks of life.

Addressing the Opposition

Nyla's campaign faced significant opposition from conservative factions in Qirona. However, she did not let this deter her. Nyla approached the opposition with empathy, engaging in respectful debates and conversations. She sought to challenge misconceptions and stereotypes, presenting evidence and personal stories to counter prejudice. Through her compassionate approach, Nyla was able to build bridges and change hearts and minds.

Promoting Policy Change

Nyla's campaign went beyond awareness-raising, actively advocating for policy change. She lobbied lawmakers, participated in public hearings, and rallied public support for LGBTQ-inclusive legislation. Nyla's campaign achieved several policy victories, including anti-discrimination laws, healthcare reforms, and legal recognition for same-sex partnerships. These legislative milestones marked a significant shift towards a more inclusive and equal society.

Unconventional Approach: The Rainbow Challenge

One unconventional yet highly effective aspect of Nyla's campaign was the Rainbow Challenge. Inspired by the viral ice bucket challenge, Nyla initiated a movement where participants would wear rainbow-colored accessories for a day, symbolizing their support for LGBTQ rights. This simple act sparked conversations nationwide, generating widespread visibility and empathy for the LGBTQ community.

Exercises

1. Research a historical figure who has made significant contributions to LGBTQ rights and present their story in a creative format, such as a poem or a short play.
2. Write an imaginary dialogue between Nyla Ashen and a prominent LGBTQ activist from another country discussing their respective campaigns and the challenges they face.
3. Explore the impact of LGBTQ media representation on societal attitudes and write an essay on its importance.
4. Create a social media campaign promoting LGBTQ rights, using hashtags and visual content to engage and educate your audience.
5. Formulate a plan for an LGBTQ-inclusive policy at your school or workplace, outlining the key steps and strategies required for successful implementation.

Conclusion

Nyla Ashen's groundbreaking LGBTQ campaign pushed the boundaries of acceptance and created a society that celebrated diversity. Through a combination of awareness-raising, collaboration, policy advocacy, and creative strategies, Nyla's campaign transformed the landscape of LGBTQ rights in Qirona. Her relentless efforts inspired individuals, changed hearts and minds, and paved the way for a more inclusive future. The Rainbow Challenge, in particular, showcased the power of unconventional approaches in effecting change. Nyla's campaign serves as a shining example of the impact that passionate advocacy can have on the world.

Facing Opposition and Backlash

In Nyla Ashen's fight for LGBTQ rights in Qirona, she faced intense opposition and backlash from various groups and individuals who resisted the idea of acceptance and equality. This section explores the challenges Nyla encountered and how she navigated through them with resilience and determination.

The Religious Backlash

One of the major sources of opposition Nyla faced came from religious groups who believed that homosexuality was against their faith. They argued that LGBTQ individuals were deviating from traditional values and norms.

To address this issue, Nyla adopted a proactive approach by engaging in dialogue with religious leaders and communities. She emphasized the importance of love, compassion, and respecting the dignity of every individual, regardless of their sexual orientation or gender identity. Nyla emphasized that LGBTQ rights were not in conflict with religious beliefs but rather a call for inclusivity and acceptance within faith communities. By highlighting stories of LGBTQ individuals who held religious beliefs, she aimed to challenge the perception that being LGBTQ and religious were mutually exclusive.

Political Resistance

Nyla faced political resistance from lawmakers who were hesitant to pass LGBTQ-inclusive legislation. Many politicians feared backlash from conservative constituents and faced pressure from lobbying groups that opposed LGBTQ rights.

In response, Nyla used her platform to educate lawmakers through presentations, workshops, and meetings. She presented evidence that highlighted the positive impact of LGBTQ rights on society, including improved mental health outcomes for LGBTQ individuals and the economic benefits of LGBTQ-inclusive policies.

To gain support from the public and put pressure on politicians, Nyla organized peaceful protests and marches, amplifying the voices of LGBTQ individuals and their allies. By mobilizing a strong and visible movement, she created a sense of urgency and highlighted the demands for equal rights.

Social Stigma and Discrimination

Nyla faced significant social stigma and discrimination throughout her activism journey. Homophobic and transphobic individuals targeted her with hate speech, online harassment, and even physical threats. This backlash took a toll on her mental health and well-being.

To combat this, Nyla leaned on her support network of friends, family, and fellow activists. She advocated for mental health resources and support for LGBTQ individuals facing similar challenges. Nyla also found solace in art and music, using her creativity as an outlet for self-expression and emotional release.

Recognizing the power of empathy and storytelling, Nyla shared her own experiences and those of other LGBTQ individuals who had faced similar discrimination. Through heartfelt speeches and personal narratives, she aimed to break down societal biases and bridge the gap of understanding.

Navigating the Backlash

In navigating the opposition and backlash, Nyla developed strategies to overcome obstacles while staying true to her vision of a more inclusive society.

One of her key strategies was collaboration and coalition-building. Nyla sought partnerships with other social justice movements, recognizing the interconnected nature of various forms of discrimination. By working together, they amplified their collective voices and created a united front against discrimination.

Another strategy was using humor and wit to disarm her opponents. Nyla employed satire, irony, and sarcasm to challenge stereotypes and misconceptions about LGBTQ individuals. Through witty comebacks and clever responses, she redirected negative energy and shifted the narrative in a more positive and inclusive direction.

It is important to note that facing opposition and backlash is an ongoing challenge for LGBTQ activists like Nyla Ashen. However, through her resilience, determination, and strategic approach, Nyla brought significant change to Qirona's LGBTQ landscape, paving the way for a more accepting and inclusive future.

Unconventional Insight: One unconventional yet effective approach that Nyla used to combat opposition was through artivism. Nyla collaborated with LGBTQ artists and creatives to create thought-provoking exhibits, performances, and installations that challenged societal norms and provoked conversations about LGBTQ rights. These artistic expressions acted as powerful tools for change, transcending language barriers, and engaging with the audience at an emotional and visceral level.

Example: One of Nyla's notable collaborations was with a renowned street artist, who created vibrant murals celebrating LGBTQ identities and love. These murals transformed once-blank walls into colorful symbols of hope and pride, sparking conversations and creating a sense of belonging within the community. This unconventional form of activism not only beautified the city but also challenged prejudices and sparked important conversations about acceptance and equality.

The Power of Allies in Nyla's Fight

Nyla Ashen's journey as an LGBTQ activist was not one she embarked on alone. Throughout her fight for equality and acceptance, she recognized the power of allies in amplifying her voice and effecting real change in the community. In this section, we will explore the significance of allies in Nyla's fight and how their support played a crucial role in advancing LGBTQ rights in Qirona.

Understanding the Role of Allies

Allies are individuals who are not necessarily part of the LGBTQ community but actively support and advocate for LGBTQ rights. They recognize the importance of inclusivity, and their involvement contributes to a more inclusive society. Nyla Ashen understood that building a strong coalition of allies was essential to breaking LGBTQ barriers in Qirona.

The Impact of Allyship on Nyla's Advocacy

Nyla's allies played a pivotal role in her advocacy efforts. By lending their support, they helped increase the visibility and reach of her campaigns, making it more difficult for discriminatory forces to ignore. This broader coalition also allowed for a diversity of perspectives and experiences, strengthening Nyla's cause and fostering a sense of unity within the LGBTQ community.

Creating Safe Spaces

Allies, whether individuals or organizations, were instrumental in creating safe spaces for LGBTQ individuals in Qirona. Through their own platforms, they provided resources and platforms for personal stories and experiences to be shared, creating a sense of belonging and empowerment. These safe spaces allowed LGBTQ individuals to speak their truth and helped break down barriers of fear and discrimination.

Amplifying LGBTQ Voices

One of the key roles allies played in Nyla's fight was the amplification of LGBTQ voices. They used their platforms, influence, and privilege to elevate the narratives and concerns of the LGBTQ community. By doing so, they helped drive societal change and challenge existing biases and stereotypes. Allies helped bridge the gap between the LGBTQ community and those who may not understand or fully grasp their lived experiences.

Educating and Encouraging Dialogue

Allies also played a crucial role in educating others and sparking important conversations surrounding LGBTQ issues. They served as educators, using their knowledge and understanding to dispel myths and misconceptions about the LGBTQ community. By encouraging dialogue, they facilitated a deeper understanding and empathy, enabling others to become more supportive and inclusive.

Challenges and Opportunities for Allyship

While allyship was powerful in Nyla's fight, it was not without challenges. Allies faced backlash and opposition from those resistant to change. However, their unwavering commitment to the cause strengthened Nyla's movement and inspired others to join in advocating for LGBTQ rights.

To be effective allies, individuals and organizations must commit to ongoing education, introspection, and self-improvement. They must actively listen to the LGBTQ community and respect their leadership. The power of allies lies in their willingness to learn, unlearn, and challenge their own biases.

Unconventional But Relevant - The Power of Comedy

Nyla's campaign also benefitted from an unconventional but highly effective strategy - the power of comedy. Allies in the entertainment industry recognized the role humor plays in breaking down barriers and fostering understanding. Through comedy sketches, satirical videos, and humorous performances, they challenged societal norms and sparked conversations about LGBTQ issues in an approachable manner.

By using humor to tackle sensitive subjects, allies helped create a more inclusive and accepting environment. Laughter often serves as a bridge between communities, allowing them to find common ground and empathize with experiences different from their own. Nyla and her allies harnessed this power, leveraging comedy as a tool to connect with people, educate them, and encourage positive change.

Conclusion

In her fight for LGBTQ rights in Qirona, Nyla Ashen recognized the invaluable role of allies. Their support, amplification of LGBTQ voices, creation of safe spaces, and dedication to education propelled her advocacy efforts forward. Despite challenges, allies remained steadfast in their commitment to change, working alongside Nyla to break down barriers and promote acceptance. Through their collective efforts, they brought the LGBTQ community closer to achieving equality and inspired future generations to continue fighting for the rights and dignity of all individuals, regardless of sexual orientation or gender identity.

Overcoming obstacles with humor and wit

In her journey as an LGBTQ activist, Nyla Ashen faced numerous obstacles and challenges. However, she tackled them with a unique approach that combined humor and wit. Nyla believed that laughter and cleverness could be powerful tools in breaking down barriers and challenging societal norms. In this section, we will explore how Nyla overcame obstacles with her sharp sense of humor and quick wit.

The power of humor in advocacy

Nyla understood the power of humor to disarm her opponents and make her message more accessible to a wider audience. She recognized that making people laugh could create a connection and open their minds to new perspectives. Nyla used satire, sarcasm, and clever wordplay to address sensitive topics, challenging stereotypes and prejudices in a lighthearted way.

Crafting witty comebacks

One of Nyla's greatest strengths was her ability to respond to criticism and negativity with grace and wit. Instead of reacting defensively, Nyla would often respond with a well-crafted and clever comeback, disarming her critics and turning the situation into an opportunity for dialogue. Her quick thinking and sharp tongue often left her opponents speechless, while her supporters found inspiration in her ability to eloquently defend her beliefs.

Using humor to build bridges

Nyla recognized that humor could also be a powerful tool to bridge divides and bring people together. She often used self-deprecating humor to put others at ease and foster understanding. By making light of her own experiences and challenging stereotypes, Nyla encouraged conversations that sparked empathy and a shared sense of humanity. Her ability to find common ground with those who held opposing views helped to create a platform for constructive dialogue and change.

Addressing serious issues with levity

While Nyla's humorous approach was effective in engaging a wide audience, she never lost sight of the seriousness of the issues she was fighting for. Through her unique blend of wit and empathy, she managed to navigate the fine line between addressing the gravity of LGBTQ struggles and using humor to create awareness and change. Nyla's ability to infuse levity into heavy topics enabled her to connect with individuals who may have been hesitant to delve into these issues.

Challenges and misconceptions

There were, of course, challenges and misconceptions that Nyla faced when utilizing humor and wit in her activism. Some critics accused her of not taking the LGBTQ cause seriously or trivializing the struggles of the community. However, Nyla understood that her approach was a means to an end. By drawing attention with her clever and humorous style, she could then use that platform to educate and advocate for change.

Unconventional yet relevant approach

Nyla's unconventional approach to tackling LGBTQ barriers with humor and wit may have raised eyebrows initially, but it ultimately proved to be effective. It allowed her to reach a broader audience, dismantle stereotypes, and foster dialogue around LGBTQ rights. Her ability to navigate serious issues with levity and address criticism with sharp comebacks made her a force to be reckoned with in the advocacy world.

Exercise: Using humor in advocacy

Think about an issue that you are passionate about and brainstorm ways in which you can employ humor to advocate for change. Consider the stereotypes and misconceptions surrounding the topic and how humor can be used to challenge them. Write down one humorous statement or clever comeback that you could use to address criticism or engage with individuals who hold opposing views.

Additional Resources

1. "The Power of Humor in Social Activism" by TEDx Talks: This insightful TED Talk explores the role of humor in social activism and provides examples of successful advocates who effectively used humor to drive change.

2. "Funny or Die: The Importance of Humor in Advocacy" by HuffPost: This article examines the ways in which humor can be used to create awareness, challenge norms, and advocate for various causes.

3. "How to Use Wit and Humor to Advocate for Change" by The Conversation: This resource offers practical tips and advice on leveraging humor to overcome obstacles and effect meaningful change.

Remember, while humor can be a powerful tool, it's important to strike a balance and ensure that the message and intent behind the humor are clear. Always approach sensitive topics with respect and empathy, using humor as a means to open conversations rather than shutting them down.

Nyla's successful campaign milestones

Nyla Ashen's journey as an LGBTQ activist has been marked by numerous significant milestones that have propelled her message of equality and acceptance forward. Through her tireless efforts, she has shattered barriers and made a lasting impact on the LGBTQ community in Qirona. Let's dive into some of Nyla's most successful campaign milestones.

One of Nyla's earliest campaign milestones was advocating for LGBTQ-inclusive policies in educational institutions. Recognizing the importance of education in shaping attitudes and fostering acceptance, Nyla worked relentlessly to promote LGBTQ-inclusive curricula and safe school environments. She collaborated with educators, administrators, and LGBTQ youth organizations to develop guidelines for inclusive education that were eventually adopted by several schools across Qirona.

In one particularly groundbreaking achievement, Nyla successfully spearheaded the implementation of gender-neutral restrooms in public spaces. She tirelessly campaigned for the rights of transgender and non-binary individuals to have safe and accessible restroom facilities that aligned with their gender identity. Her efforts led to the passage of legislation that mandated the inclusion of gender-neutral restrooms in all public buildings, setting a precedent for other regions to follow.

Nyla's effective use of social media as a tool for advocacy cannot be overlooked. She harnessed the power of viral moments to bring attention to LGBTQ rights and issues. One of her most impactful social media campaigns involved sharing personal stories of discrimination and resilience from individuals within the LGBTQ community. By amplifying these voices, Nyla created a powerful platform for awareness and empathy, igniting conversations and prompting change.

A notable milestone in Nyla's campaign was her collaboration with LGBTQ influencers. She recognized the power of collective action and formed alliances with prominent LGBTQ personalities who shared her vision of a more inclusive society. Together, they organized online campaigns, events, and fundraisers to raise awareness and support for LGBTQ rights. Their collective reach had a significant impact on challenging societal norms and pushing for greater acceptance.

Nyla's ability to engage in meaningful dialogue with political leaders and policymakers was another key milestone. She actively sought opportunities to discuss LGBTQ rights and influence government decision-making. Through her eloquence and determination, Nyla successfully lobbied for legislative changes that protected LGBTQ individuals from discrimination in employment, housing, and public services. Her persuasive arguments and unwavering commitment to equality helped shape new laws and policies that transformed the lives of countless people.

These are just a few examples of Nyla Ashen's successful campaign milestones. Her unwavering dedication to the LGBTQ cause and her ability to mobilize support and effect change have made her a true trailblazer. By challenging societal norms and breaking down barriers, Nyla has left an indelible mark on the LGBTQ community in Qirona and beyond. Her accomplishments serve as a source of inspiration for future activists, reminding us all of the potential for progress and acceptance.

Section Two

The Impact of Media on Nyla's Activism

The media played a crucial role in shaping Nyla Ashen's activism journey in Qirona. Through various platforms, Nyla effectively spread awareness, challenged stereotypes, and amplified the voices of the LGBTQ community. In this section, we will explore the profound impact of media on Nyla's journey, from her presence in TV interviews and talk shows to her viral social media moments.

Harnessing the Power of TV Interviews and Talk Shows

Nyla Ashen's presence in TV interviews and talk shows served as a powerful platform for discussing LGBTQ rights and dismantling harmful narratives. With her eloquence and compelling storytelling, Nyla captured the attention of millions, using her platform to educate and inspire.

One memorable TV interview took place on "The Talk," a popular daytime show. Nyla delivered a heartfelt speech, sharing personal stories of discrimination and bravery. This segment garnered immense media attention, leading to increased awareness and support for LGBTQ rights in Qirona.

In another memorable talk show appearance, Nyla participated in a candid discussion on "Equality Matters," a show dedicated to promoting equality and inclusivity. Nyla engaged in meaningful conversations, dispelling misconceptions about the LGBTQ community and enlightening viewers about the importance of acceptance and understanding.

Viral Social Media Moments

Nyla Ashen was no stranger to the power of social media. In fact, her viral moments on platforms like Twitter and Instagram became catalysts for change and mobilized a diverse audience. Nyla's ability to harness the essence of LGBTQ struggles and triumphs in short, impactful messages created a ripple effect that resonated with people worldwide.

One significant viral moment was when Nyla shared a personal story about her journey as a transgender woman on Twitter using the hashtag #TransIsBeautiful. Her heartfelt message, coupled with an empowering photo, quickly gained traction and sparked a global conversation about transgender visibility and acceptance.

On Instagram, Nyla utilized the platform's visual nature to showcase the strength and diversity of the LGBTQ community. Through captivating photos and empowering captions, she challenged societal norms and encouraged her followers to embrace their authentic selves. Her posts often featured collaborations with LGBTQ influencers, highlighting the importance of unity and solidarity within the community.

The Importance of Representation in the Media

Nyla Ashen recognized the power of representation in the media and leveraged it to reshape societal perceptions of the LGBTQ community. By ensuring accurate and positive portrayals, Nyla aimed to normalize LGBTQ identities and increase empathy from the general public.

Nyla actively collaborated with LGBTQ influencers across various social media platforms, promoting a wide range of LGBTQ experiences. These collaborations showcased the diversity within the community, breaking down stereotypes and fostering a sense of belonging for individuals who had previously felt marginalized.

To further uplift LGBTQ voices, Nyla actively engaged with mainstream media outlets to advocate for authentic representation. She emphasized the need for diverse storytelling, ensuring that LGBTQ characters and narratives were portrayed with nuance and respect. Through her efforts, Nyla played a vital role in pushing for LGBTQ-inclusive storylines in popular TV shows and movies.

Navigating and Overcoming Media Challenges

Navigating the media landscape as an LGBTQ activist was not without its challenges for Nyla Ashen. She faced both misconceptions and outright hostility from certain media outlets. However, she always found creative ways to address adversity and turn it into an opportunity for education and growth.

In response to negative coverage or misrepresentation, Nyla employed humor and wit to diffuse prejudice and challenge stereotypes. Through her quick thinking and sharp tongue, she effectively countered biased narratives, providing a fresh perspective on LGBTQ issues.

One notable example occurred during a radio interview with a conservative host known for his anti-LGBTQ agenda. Instead of engaging in a heated debate, Nyla used humor to navigate the conversation, highlighting the absurdity of the host's arguments while still conveying essential messages of acceptance and equality.

Amplifying LGBTQ Voices through Collaborations

In addition to her collaborations with LGBTQ influencers, Nyla Ashen also worked closely with LGBTQ celebrities to amplify the voices of the community. By joining forces with well-known figures, she harnessed their platforms to reach a wider audience and effect change on a larger scale.

Through strategic partnerships, Nyla advocated for LGBTQ rights alongside prominent actors, musicians, and activists. These alliances not only boosted visibility but also created a sense of unity among people from all walks of life. Together, they sent a powerful message of acceptance and inclusivity, showing that LGBTQ issues are not isolated but concern all of society.

Overall, media played an instrumental role in Nyla Ashen's activism journey. Through TV interviews, talk shows, viral social media moments, and collaborations, Nyla harnessed the power of media to challenge stereotypes, provoke conversations, and increase LGBTQ visibility. Her creative navigation of media challenges and commitment to authentic representation propelled her fight for equality forward, leaving an indelible impact on Qirona and inspiring future generations to continue the struggle for acceptance and understanding.

Nyla's presence in TV interviews and talk shows

Nyla Ashen's journey as an LGBTQ activist has been amplified by her presence in TV interviews and talk shows. With her eloquence and powerful message, she has captivated audiences worldwide, spreading awareness and advocating for LGBTQ rights. Let's delve into the impact of Nyla's television appearances and how they have influenced her activism.

Connecting with the Masses

Nyla's television interviews have given her a platform to connect with a diverse audience, reaching beyond the LGBTQ community. Her ability to articulate her experiences and challenges has touched the hearts and minds of people from all walks of life.

In interviews, Nyla shares personal stories that humanize the struggles faced by LGBTQ individuals, making her message relatable. She emphasizes the importance of empathy and understanding, encouraging viewers to consider the discrimination and obstacles faced by the LGBTQ community.

One example of Nyla's impactful TV appearance was on "The Melissa Thompson Show," where she shared her journey of self-discovery and the difficulties she encountered along the way. By speaking openly and honestly about the challenges she faced, Nyla was able to inspire viewers to question their own prejudices and support LGBTQ rights.

Promoting Dialogue and Education

TV interviews and talk shows have provided Nyla with opportunities to educate the public about LGBTQ issues. Nyla takes advantage of these platforms to dispel myths and misunderstandings surrounding the community, fostering a more inclusive and accepting society.

During interviews, Nyla highlights the importance of comprehensive sex education that includes LGBTQ topics. She discusses the dire need for schools to address the unique experiences and challenges faced by LGBTQ students, ensuring their well-being and equal treatment.

An exceptional example of Nyla's influence in promoting dialogue was her appearance on "The Spectrum Show," where she engaged in a respectful conversation with individuals holding opposing viewpoints. Nyla's calm yet assertive demeanor encouraged meaningful discussions on LGBTQ rights and challenged prejudices, leaving a positive impact on viewers.

Utilizing Humor and Wit

Nyla's television presence is not limited to serious discussions; she also utilizes humor and wit to engage with her audience. By infusing her interviews with light-hearted banter and relatable anecdotes, Nyla creates an approachable image that breaks down barriers and fosters connection.

In one memorable talk show appearance on "Late Night with Emma Fairfield," Nyla charmed the audience with her quick wit and comedic timing. She skillfully used humor as a tool to humanize the LGBTQ experience, making it more accessible to a wider audience. Nyla's ability to find common ground through laughter opened up conversations about acceptance and understanding.

Inspiring Future Advocates

Nyla's presence on TV interviews and talk shows has inspired countless individuals worldwide to become LGBTQ activists themselves. Her poise, eloquence, and unwavering determination have become a beacon of hope for LGBTQ youth, encouraging them to pursue change in their own communities.

By openly discussing her own struggles and triumphs, Nyla instills courage and resilience in those who may be facing similar challenges. Through her interviews, she communicates the message that change is possible and that every individual has the power to make a difference.

Nyla's interview on "The Catalyst Effect" resonated deeply with viewers, especially LGBTQ youth, who expressed gratitude for her unwavering advocacy. Her passion and authenticity have motivated a new generation to pick up the torch and continue to push for LGBTQ rights.

A Uniquely Impactful Journey

Nyla Ashen's television interviews and talk show appearances form an integral part of her journey as an LGBTQ activist. Through these platforms, she has connected with a diverse audience, promoted dialogue and education, utilized humor and wit, and inspired future advocates.

Nyla's television presence has not only elevated her activism but also helped bring LGBTQ issues into the mainstream conversation. Her unwavering determination to effect change and create a more accepting world has left an indelible mark on society. As Nyla continues to influence and inspire, her presence in TV interviews and talk shows will continue to amplify the voices of the LGBTQ community and pave the way for a more inclusive future.

Nyla's Viral Social Media Moments

Nyla Ashen's journey as an LGBTQ activist has been fueled, in large part, by her ability to connect with people through the power of social media. With her unique blend of humor, wit, and vulnerability, Nyla has captivated audiences across the globe, sparking conversations, and challenging societal norms. In this section, we explore some of Nyla's most memorable viral social media moments and their impact on the LGBTQ community.

Spreading Awareness with #ProudToBeMe

One of Nyla's breakthrough social media campaigns was the hashtag #ProudToBeMe, which aimed to empower individuals to embrace their true selves unapologetically. Nyla initiated this movement by sharing her own personal journey of self-discovery, accompanied by a heartfelt message encouraging others to do the same.

The campaign quickly gained momentum as people from all walks of life shared their stories, struggles, and triumphs using the hashtag. Nyla's genuine authenticity and relatability resonated deeply with LGBTQ individuals and allies, fostering a sense of community and solidarity. The hashtag went viral, with millions of posts flooding social media platforms, creating a powerful visual representation of the diverse LGBTQ experiences worldwide.

Sparking Dialogue with "Ask Nyla"

Nyla recognized the importance of creating an open dialogue and dispelling misconceptions surrounding the LGBTQ community. To facilitate this, she launched a video series on her social media channels titled "Ask Nyla," where she would answer questions posed by her followers.

The series became an instant hit, as Nyla fearlessly tackled a wide range of topics, from coming out experiences and self-acceptance to LGBTQ rights and intersectionality. Her honest and straightforward approach made complex issues accessible to a broader audience, encouraging empathy, understanding, and sparking meaningful conversations within and outside the LGBTQ community.

Meme Magic: Nyla's Humor as a Weapon

Nyla has an innate talent for using humor to drive her message home. She leverages the power of memes and viral trends to educate and uplift her audience, challenging societal norms through clever satire.

By creating witty and relatable content, Nyla has turned unpleasant or uncomfortable situations faced by the LGBTQ community into moments of reflection and realization. Her humor acts both as an escape from the hardships faced by many and as a catalyst for social change.

Using Livestreams to Connect and Empower

Livestreaming platforms have allowed Nyla to connect with her followers in real-time, fostering a sense of intimacy and community. Through these streams, she addresses current issues, provides support and advice, and shares stories of resilience and hope.

Nyla's live Q&A sessions have become a safe space for LGBTQ individuals to seek guidance and solace. By sharing her own experiences and offering heartfelt advice, she has inspired countless viewers to embrace their identities and fight for their rights.

The Power of Storytelling: Nyla's Short Films

In addition to her online presence, Nyla has also utilized the power of visual storytelling to shed light on LGBTQ experiences. Through short films, she has captured the raw emotions and challenges faced by individuals within the community.

These poignant narratives serve as powerful tools for empathy and education, challenging societal biases, and fostering a more inclusive world. By showcasing the diversity of LGBTQ stories, Nyla encourages viewers to recognize the humanity in each individual and to celebrate the beauty of their differences.

The Unconventional Call to Action

Beyond the usual engagement tactics, Nyla has embarked on unconventional initiatives to raise awareness and incite change. One such endeavor was the creation of an LGBTQ-themed mobile game, designed to educate players about the challenges faced by the community while promoting empathy and understanding.

This innovative approach combined entertainment with activism, reaching a wider audience that may not have been directly engaged with LGBTQ issues. Through the game, players experienced the struggles and triumphs of LGBTQ individuals, challenging their own biases and fostering a greater sense of empathy.

Conclusion

Nyla Ashen's viral social media moments have become a powerful force for change in the LGBTQ community. Through hashtags, Q&A sessions, humor, storytelling, and even mobile games, Nyla has leveraged the reach and interconnectedness of social media to spark dialogue, educate, and inspire millions.

Her ability to connect with individuals on a personal level has propelled her activism to new heights, making her a revered figure and role model for LGBTQ individuals worldwide. As Nyla continues to use the power of social media to advocate for equality and acceptance, her viral moments serve as a constant reminder of the immense impact one person can have on reshaping society.

The importance of representation in the media

Representation in the media plays a crucial role in shaping societal attitudes, perceptions, and understanding of the LGBTQ community. It is through the power of media that narratives are constructed, identities are formed, and stereotypes are either reinforced or challenged. In this section, we will explore the significance of representation in the media and how it has impacted the LGBTQ community.

Creating visibility and validation

One of the key reasons why representation in the media is important is its ability to create visibility for the LGBTQ community. Historically, LGBTQ individuals have been underrepresented or misrepresented in mainstream media, leading to feelings of invisibility and marginalization. By featuring LGBTQ characters, storylines, and experiences, media representation provides validation to a diverse range of identities and allows individuals to see themselves reflected in the stories they consume.

When LGBTQ people see themselves portrayed positively and authentically on screen, it can have a profound impact on their self-esteem and mental well-being. It sends a powerful message that their experiences matter and that they are not alone. Representation can also help combat the harmful effects of internalized homophobia or transphobia by challenging stereotypes and showcasing the beauty and diversity of the LGBTQ community.

Fostering empathy and understanding

Media representation also plays a crucial role in fostering empathy and understanding among the general public. When people are exposed to diverse

LGBTQ stories and characters, it humanizes the community and breaks down stereotypes and prejudices. It challenges preconceived notions and opens up avenues for dialogue and education.

Through authentic representation, media can highlight the shared experiences, struggles, and triumphs that LGBTQ individuals go through. This helps to build bridges of understanding between different communities and encourages empathy and acceptance. By portraying LGBTQ characters as multidimensional individuals with complex lives, media representation helps challenge the notion that being LGBTQ is something to fear or reject.

Breaking down barriers and challenging norms

Representation in the media has the power to challenge societal norms and break down barriers. LGBTQ characters and storylines can push the boundaries of what is considered "normal" or "acceptable" in society, allowing for the exploration of diverse narratives and identities.

By showcasing LGBTQ individuals in a variety of roles and professions, media representation helps dismantle harmful stereotypes and promotes inclusivity. For example, seeing LGBTQ characters in positions of power, such as CEOs, doctors, or political leaders, challenges the notion that being LGBTQ limits one's potential.

Moreover, representation in the media can inspire and empower LGBTQ individuals to embrace their authentic selves and pursue their dreams. When LGBTQ youth see successful and confident role models in the media, they are more likely to believe in their own abilities and future prospects.

The pitfalls of misrepresentation

While representation in the media can have a transformative impact, it is important to acknowledge the pitfalls of misrepresentation. Stereotypical or tokenistic portrayals of LGBTQ characters can perpetuate harmful stereotypes and do more harm than good. Misrepresentation can reinforce negative biases and further marginalize the LGBTQ community.

To avoid these pitfalls, media creators and storytellers must prioritize authenticity, inclusivity, and collaboration with LGBTQ individuals. It is crucial to involve LGBTQ voices at every level of the creative process, from writing and directing to casting and production. This ensures that diverse LGBTQ experiences are accurately and respectfully represented, and that harmful tropes are avoided.

Confronting biases through media

Media representation has the power to confront biases and provoke critical conversations. By illustrating the challenges faced by LGBTQ individuals – such as discrimination, violence, and barriers to healthcare – media can shine a light on the systemic issues that need to be addressed.

Furthermore, media representation can serve as a catalyst for social and political change. When LGBTQ storylines are integrated into popular shows and films, it reaches a broader audience and raises awareness of LGBTQ rights and issues. This can lead to public support for policy changes and contribute to the dismantling of discriminatory laws and practices.

An unconventional approach: LGBTQ storytelling through art

One unconventional approach to LGBTQ representation in the media is through the medium of art. Visual and performance art can be a powerful tool for expressing LGBTQ experiences and challenging societal norms. Artists often use their work to engage with LGBTQ issues and advocate for change.

For example, queer photography, paintings, and sculptures can capture the essence of LGBTQ experiences, emotions, and struggles. These artistic creations provide a platform for LGBTQ individuals to tell their stories authentically and invite viewers to empathize and reflect on their own biases and perceptions.

Similarly, LGBTQ-driven theater, dance, and music performances can illuminate the unique journeys and challenges faced by the community. By centering LGBTQ stories and experiences in their work, artists can foster a sense of belonging and pride within the community, while also inviting broader audiences to engage with and understand LGBTQ lives.

In conclusion, representation in the media holds immense power in shaping attitudes, perceptions, and understanding of the LGBTQ community. By creating visibility, fostering empathy, breaking down barriers, and confronting biases, media representation can revolutionize societal norms, challenge prejudices, and promote acceptance and equality. It is vital for media creators to prioritize authentic and inclusive portrayals of LGBTQ individuals, while also recognizing the importance of collaboration and involving LGBTQ voices in the storytelling process. Through media representation, we can create a world where everyone sees themselves represented and celebrated, regardless of their sexual orientation or gender identity.

Nyla's Collaboration with LGBTQ Influencers

Nyla Ashen's groundbreaking activism in Qirona extended beyond her own efforts. She recognized the power of collaboration and formed meaningful partnerships with influential LGBTQ individuals who shared her vision for equality and acceptance. Through these collaborations, Nyla aimed to amplify the voices of the LGBTQ community and create a united front in the fight for LGBTQ rights.

The Importance of LGBTQ Influencers

In the age of social media, influencers have a significant impact on shaping public opinion and driving social change. LGBTQ influencers, in particular, play a crucial role in raising awareness, challenging stereotypes, and fostering inclusivity.

Nyla recognized the unique position of LGBTQ influencers in reaching audiences around the world. Their personal experiences and authentic voices resonated with LGBTQ individuals, providing hope, inspiration, and a sense of belonging. By collaborating with these influencers, Nyla aimed to leverage their reach and influence to promote LGBTQ rights and advance her advocacy efforts.

Choosing the Right Collaborators

When seeking collaborations with LGBTQ influencers, Nyla focused on authenticity, shared values, and a genuine commitment to the cause. She sought out individuals who were unafraid to embrace their identities and shared their stories openly and honestly. These collaborations were not just about promoting Nyla's agenda but about creating a platform for diverse LGBTQ voices to be heard.

Nyla understood the importance of diverse representation within the LGBTQ community. She sought collaborations with influencers from different backgrounds, ethnicities, gender identities, and experiences. By highlighting the diverse narratives within the community, Nyla aimed to break down stereotypes and challenge societal norms.

Collaborative Initiatives

Nyla's collaborations with LGBTQ influencers took various forms, each designed to make a meaningful impact and foster positive change.

Social Media Campaigns: Nyla joined forces with influential LGBTQ individuals to launch powerful social media campaigns. Through hashtags, videos, and personal stories, these campaigns aimed to educate, inspire, and engage audiences worldwide. These collaborations helped raise awareness about LGBTQ issues, combat discrimination and promote acceptance.

Public Appearances and Events: Nyla and her collaborators organized public appearances, panel discussions, and events to share their experiences, insights, and advocacy work. These events brought together LGBTQ influencers, activists, and allies to discuss important topics, celebrate progress, and identify areas for further action. Nyla understood that public visibility and engagement were vital in effecting societal change.

Educational Initiatives: Nyla collaborated with LGBTQ influencers to develop educational initiatives, such as workshops, seminars, and online resources. These initiatives aimed to provide information, support, and resources for LGBTQ individuals, their families, and communities. By working together, Nyla and her collaborators empowered individuals with knowledge and tools to create inclusive environments and challenge discrimination.

Unconventional Approach: Impact Through Intersectionality

Nyla Ashen recognized that LGBTQ issues intersect with various other social justice causes, such as gender equality, racial justice, and disability rights. In her collaborations with LGBTQ influencers, she encouraged an intersectional approach to advocacy.

By collaborating with influencers from different social justice movements, Nyla sought to amplify voices and draw attention to the interconnections between different marginalized communities. This approach not only expanded the reach and impact of her activism but also fostered solidarity and collective action among various advocacy groups.

Real-Life Example: Amplifying Voices Through Collaboration

One notable example of Nyla's collaboration with LGBTQ influencers was her partnership with Mia Lopez, a transgender activist and social media influencer known for her candid and insightful content.

Nyla recognized Mia's ability to connect with younger generations and address the unique challenges faced by transgender individuals. Together, they organized a social media campaign called "Transcending Barriers," aimed at breaking down misconceptions and promoting inclusivity.

Through powerful videos and personal anecdotes, Mia shared her journey of self-discovery and resilience. This collaboration allowed Nyla and Mia to reach a wider audience, educate the public on transgender issues, and create a safe space for dialogue and understanding.

Conclusion

Collaboration with LGBTQ influencers proved to be a powerful tool in Nyla Ashen's activism. By leveraging their reach, authenticity, and diverse perspectives, Nyla aimed to create a united front in the fight for LGBTQ rights. Through social media campaigns, public appearances, and educational initiatives, Nyla and her collaborators worked together to raise awareness, challenge stereotypes, and foster inclusivity. Their collaborations served as a testament to the strength of collective action and the impact it can have on achieving social change.

Section Three

Nyla's alliance with LGBTQ celebrities

Nyla Ashen's unwavering dedication to LGBTQ rights and activism has not only made her a revered figure within the community but has also attracted the attention and support of numerous LGBTQ celebrities. Nyla's alliance with these influential figures has played a pivotal role in amplifying her message and advancing the cause of equality and acceptance.

One of the most prominent LGBTQ celebrities who has joined forces with Nyla is Ryan Hartley, a renowned actor and prominent advocate for LGBTQ rights. Ryan, known for his breakthrough role in the critically acclaimed film "Love Without Boundaries," has been a vocal supporter of Nyla's campaigns and initiatives. He has used his platform to shed light on the barriers faced by the LGBTQ community and to demand meaningful change. Together, Nyla and Ryan have embarked on joint ventures such as organizing fundraisers and awareness events to generate funds for LGBTQ organizations and support LGBTQ youth initiatives.

Another LGBTQ celebrity who has aligned with Nyla is Harper Thompson, a successful musician and LGBTQ icon. Harper's soulful music and empowering lyrics have resonated with millions around the world, transcending barriers of sexuality and inspiring people to embrace their true selves. Harper's collaboration with Nyla has led to powerful advocacy campaigns, including a celebrity-filled concert series called "Proud Harmonies," where LGBTQ artists perform to raise awareness and funds for LGBTQ causes.

But Nyla's alliance with LGBTQ celebrities doesn't stop there. She has also formed strong partnerships with high-profile figures such as Jenna Martinez, a popular TV host and LGBTQ rights advocate, and Taylor Ford, a celebrated fashion designer and LGBTQ ally. These collaborations have not only helped raise the profile of LGBTQ issues but have also provided Nyla with a diverse range of perspectives and expertise to further her activism.

Nyla's alliance with LGBTQ celebrities is not solely about garnering media attention or boosting her own fame. It is rooted in the understanding that celebrities have a unique ability to influence public opinion and shape cultural narratives. By joining forces with these influential individuals, Nyla aims to create a powerful collective voice for change and to challenge societal norms that perpetuate discrimination.

However, just like any partnership, Nyla's alliances with LGBTQ celebrities have also faced challenges and controversies. From rumors of romantic relationships to disagreements on certain advocacy strategies, the spotlight on Nyla's personal life has at times overshadowed her activism. Despite these obstacles, she remains steadfast in her commitment to the cause and continues to use her alliances to drive positive change.

In her quest for LGBTQ equality, Nyla Ashen understands that visibility, representation, and the collaboration of influential figures are key components of effecting lasting change. By joining forces with LGBTQ celebrities, she not only amplifies her message but also fosters a sense of unity and hope within the LGBTQ community. Nyla's alliances not only enrich her journey but also inspire countless LGBTQ individuals to believe in a future where love and acceptance triumph over discrimination.

The significance of LGBTQ representation in the entertainment industry

The entertainment industry has the power to shape societal attitudes and beliefs, making it a crucial platform for promoting LGBTQ rights and visibility. LGBTQ representation in the media allows for greater understanding, acceptance, and empathy towards the community. In this section, we will explore the profound impact of LGBTQ representation in the entertainment industry, from increasing visibility to challenging stereotypes and fostering inclusivity.

Increasing Visibility

LGBTQ representation in the entertainment industry has played a pivotal role in providing much-needed visibility to queer individuals. By featuring diverse LGBTQ characters and storylines, television shows, movies, and music open up opportunities for viewers to connect with and relate to LGBTQ experiences. This representation helps validate the lived experiences of LGBTQ individuals and allows them to see their stories reflected on screen.

For instance, the hit TV show "Queer Eye" has gained international acclaim for its positive portrayal of LGBTQ individuals. The heartwarming interactions between the Fab Five and their makeover subjects challenge stereotypes and showcase the diverse talents and strengths of LGBTQ individuals.

Challenging Stereotypes

LGBTQ representation in the entertainment industry has been instrumental in breaking down harmful stereotypes and misconceptions surrounding the community. By showcasing multifaceted LGBTQ characters, media depictions challenge the narrow definitions and assumptions often associated with sexual orientation and gender identity.

For example, the critically acclaimed show "Pose" celebrates the vibrant ballroom culture and the lives of transgender individuals. Through compelling storytelling and nuanced character development, the series challenges preconceived notions about trans identities, giving viewers a deeper understanding of the diverse experiences within the LGBTQ community.

Fostering Inclusivity

LGBTQ representation in the entertainment industry has the power to foster inclusivity and create a sense of belonging for marginalized communities. By featuring LGBTQ characters and stories, media content helps LGBTQ individuals feel represented, acknowledged, and accepted.

The movie "Love, Simon," based on the novel by Becky Albertalli, brought a heartfelt LGBTQ love story to the mainstream. The film resonated with audiences of all backgrounds, opening up conversations about acceptance, self-identity, and the importance of LGBTQ representation in the entertainment industry.

Challenges and Opportunities

While LGBTQ representation in the entertainment industry has come a long way, there are still challenges that need to be addressed. One such challenge is the issue of token representation, where LGBTQ characters are often reduced to stereotypes or appear as one-dimensional sidekicks.

To ensure more authentic and diverse LGBTQ representation, it is crucial for industry gatekeepers, such as producers, directors, and writers, to include queer voices behind the scenes. By employing LGBTQ creators and consultants, the industry can avoid perpetuating harmful stereotypes and foster accurate and meaningful representation.

Moreover, it is essential to create opportunities for LGBTQ artists to tell their own stories and shape the narrative surrounding their experiences. This can be accomplished through initiatives that support and amplify LGBTQ voices, providing platforms for their creative expression and allowing for authentic storytelling.

Conclusion

LGBTQ representation in the entertainment industry has immense significance in promoting acceptance, understanding, and equality. By increasing visibility, challenging stereotypes, and fostering inclusivity, media content plays a vital role in shaping societal attitudes towards the LGBTQ community.

As consumers and creators of media, we have the power to support and demand more LGBTQ representation in the entertainment industry. Through our collective efforts, we can continue to create a more inclusive and equitable world for LGBTQ individuals.

Rumors and controversies surrounding Nyla's relationships

Throughout her journey as an LGBTQ activist, Nyla Ashen has faced not only the challenges of fighting for equality and acceptance but also the scrutiny and gossip surrounding her personal relationships. As a public figure, Nyla's love life has often been under the microscope, subject to rumors, controversies, and invasive speculation from the media and the public. In this section, we delve into some of the key instances where Nyla's relationships became the center of attention, highlighting the impact of these rumors on her activism and personal life.

The Power of Love and Support

Nyla Ashen firmly believes that love knows no boundaries or restrictions. Her relationships, like any other individual's, have been shaped by genuine connections, personal growth, and shared values. However, in the public eye, her romantic involvements have often been sensationalized and twisted to fit certain narratives.

Despite the rumors and controversies surrounding her relationships, Nyla has consistently emphasized the importance of love, understanding, and support. She has openly celebrated her partners and credited them for being pillars of strength during her activism. In doing so, Nyla challenges the perception that being an activist requires sacrificing personal happiness or compromising intimate connections.

Navigating Media Speculation

The media frenzy surrounding Nyla's relationships intensifies the challenges she faces as a public figure. Tabloids and gossip columns continually speculate about her personal life, constructing narratives that sell stories rather than presenting factual information. From alleged secret romances to exaggerated accounts of breakups, the media hype often obscures the truth and fuels unnecessary drama.

To counter this, Nyla has maintained a dignified approach. She consistently advocates for responsible journalism and urges the media to focus on her work as an activist rather than indulging in speculative gossip. By focusing on substantive discussions, Nyla seeks to redirect the narrative surrounding her relationships back towards her advocacy for LGBTQ rights.

Confronting Homophobia and Biphobia

As an openly bisexual activist, Nyla Ashen has faced not only the challenges of biphobia within the LGBTQ community but also the prejudices and stereotypes imposed by society at large. Often, rumors surrounding her relationships have been used to question her sexual orientation, perpetuating harmful misconceptions.

Nyla's response to these controversies speaks volumes about her unwavering commitment to authenticity and self-acceptance. By openly acknowledging and embracing her bisexuality, she challenges society's rigid binary notions of sexuality. Nyla stands firm in asserting that her relationships are not a spectacle or a tool for debate but a testament to her own journey of self-discovery and love.

Celebrating Healthy Relationships

In the face of rumors and controversies, Nyla Ashen continues to celebrate healthy relationships as a source of strength and inspiration. She consistently emphasizes the importance of empathy, communication, and respect within intimate connections, highlighting these values as essential for personal growth and well-being.

By sharing her experiences and insights, Nyla aims to empower others, particularly young LGBTQ individuals, to embrace their identities and pursue healthy relationships free from judgment and prejudice. Her ability to navigate rumors and controversies surrounding her relationships while maintaining her unwavering commitment to love and activism has made her a role model for many.

Breaking Barriers, Inspiring Change

Despite the unfounded rumors and controversies that have surrounded Nyla's relationships, it is important to remember her primary contributions as an LGBTQ activist. Nyla's work has broken down barriers, challenged discriminatory laws, and inspired change, both nationally and internationally.

While her relationships may attract attention, it is crucial not to lose sight of the broader impact Nyla has had on the LGBTQ community. Her unwavering advocacy and resilience in the face of adversity have made her a beacon of hope, demonstrating that love and activism can coexist and that personal relationships should never overshadow the fight for equality and acceptance.

In conclusion, the rumors and controversies surrounding Nyla Ashen's relationships serve as a stark reminder of the challenges faced by LGBTQ individuals in both their personal and public lives. Nyla's experiences shed light on the power dynamics at play in media representation and the importance of context in understanding intimate connections. Despite the scrutiny she endures, Nyla always redirects the focus back to her activism, emphasizing the need for love, acceptance, and understanding in the fight for LGBTQ rights.

Nyla's Inspirational Speeches and TED Talks

Nyla Ashen's ability to connect with audiences through her powerful speeches and thought-provoking TED talks has been instrumental in spreading awareness and creating a positive change for the LGBTQ community. Her speeches are the perfect blend of personal anecdotes, statistical data, and inspirational messages that resonate with people from diverse backgrounds. In this section, we explore some of Nyla's most impactful speeches and TED talks, analyzing her unique approach to delivering a powerful message.

Emotional Stories and Personal Anecdotes

One of Nyla's strengths as a speaker lies in her ability to share personal stories that touch the hearts of her listeners. By opening up about her own experiences as an LGBTQ individual, she creates a sense of empathy and relatability. In her TED talk titled "Love Beyond Labels," Nyla shares the emotional journey of coming out to her family and the challenges she faced along the way. She emphasizes the importance of love and acceptance, urging her audience to look beyond societal labels and embrace each other's uniqueness.

Nyla's personal anecdotes serve as powerful reminders that LGBTQ rights are not just a political issue but a deeply personal one. By humanizing the struggles and triumphs of the LGBTQ community, she encourages empathy and understanding among her listeners, fostering a more inclusive society.

Data-driven Approach

In addition to sharing personal stories, Nyla often incorporates statistical data and research findings into her speeches. By presenting evidence-backed arguments, she adds credibility to her message and persuades skeptics to reconsider their preconceived notions. In her speech "Breaking LGBTQ Barriers," Nyla cites studies and statistics that highlight the discrimination and inequality faced by the LGBTQ community. She presents compelling evidence to debunk common myths and misconceptions, challenging her audience to confront their biases and become advocates for change.

By combining emotional storytelling with factual evidence, Nyla captivates her audience and prompts them to reflect on the gravity of the issues at hand. Her data-driven approach ensures that her speeches have a lasting impact beyond the initial emotional response, encouraging individuals to take action and support LGBTQ rights.

Interactive and Engaging Presentations

Nyla's speeches and TED talks are far from mundane monologues. She understands the importance of engaging her audience and creating an interactive experience. Through the use of multimedia elements, audience participation, and thought-provoking activities, Nyla ensures that her message resonates long after the applause has faded.

In her TED talk "Unleashing LGBTQ Potential," Nyla breaks from the traditional speaker-audience dynamic by incorporating interactive exercises that encourage self-reflection. Through these activities, she prompts her listeners to examine their own biases, question societal norms, and envision a future where LGBTQ individuals can thrive without fear of discrimination. By actively involving her audience, Nyla fosters a sense of collective responsibility, inspiring individuals to become catalysts for change within their own communities.

Overcoming Adversity with Resilience and Hope

Nyla's speeches are not just about highlighting the challenges faced by the LGBTQ community; they are also about instilling hope and resilience in her listeners. Through her words of inspiration, she reminds her audience that change is possible and that unity and compassion can prevail over hatred and discrimination.

In her speech "From Darkness to Light," Nyla shares her personal journey of embracing her identity, overcoming discrimination, and finding strength in adversity. She emphasizes the importance of perseverance and self-love, urging her audience to never give up on their dreams, regardless of the obstacles they may face. Her infectious optimism and unwavering belief in a better future empower her listeners to confront their own challenges head-on and create a more inclusive world for all.

TED Talk Example: "Love Beyond Labels"

To illustrate Nyla's unique style and approach to delivering inspirational speeches, we will provide an example breakdown of her popular TED talk titled "Love Beyond Labels":

1. Introduction: - Engages the audience with a compelling opening line that sparks curiosity and captures attention. - Establishes common ground by highlighting the universal human desire for love and acceptance. - Shares a personal anecdote to create an emotional connection with the audience.

2. Personal Journey: - Opens up about the challenges of coming out as an LGBTQ individual. - Illustrates the impact of societal labels and the struggle to embrace one's true identity. - Includes stories of personal growth and self-acceptance to inspire listeners.

3. Confronting Labels: - Discusses the societal implications of labels and their impact on individuals. - Presents statistical data and research findings to challenge stereotypes and biases. - Encourages the audience to reflect on their own prejudices and assumptions.

4. The Power of Love and Acceptance: - Shares heartwarming stories of acceptance and support within the LGBTQ community. - Emphasizes the

importance of unconditional love and understanding. - Calls on the audience to embrace diversity and celebrate love beyond labels.

5. **Inspiring Action:** - Offers practical steps individuals can take to create a more inclusive society. - Encourages engagement with LGBTQ organizations and initiatives. - Calls on the audience to be allies and advocates for LGBTQ rights.

6. **Conclusion:** - Summarizes the key messages and takeaways from the talk. - Delivers a powerful closing statement that leaves a lasting impression on the audience. - Offers words of inspiration and hope for a future free from discrimination and prejudice.

Nyla Ashen's inspirational speeches and TED talks have become a catalyst for change, igniting conversations about LGBTQ rights and inspiring individuals around the world. Through her unique storytelling, data-driven approach, interactive presentations, and messages of resilience, Nyla continues to break down barriers and create a more accepting and inclusive society for all.

Nyla's Influence on LGBTQ Youth Around the World

Nyla Ashen's impact on LGBTQ youth around the world cannot be overstated. Through her advocacy work, inspiring speeches, and relatable presence in mainstream media, she has become a symbol of hope, empowerment, and resilience for countless young individuals struggling with their sexual orientation and gender identity.

1. **Fostering Representation and Visibility:** One of the key ways Nyla has influenced LGBTQ youth is by fostering representation and visibility. By being open about her own experiences and struggles, Nyla has shown young people that they are not alone. Through her media presence, Nyla has challenged stereotypes and showcased the diversity within the LGBTQ community. Her authenticity and unapologetic embrace of her identity have resonated with young individuals who often feel marginalized or invisible.

2. **Mentoring and Support:** Nyla has established mentoring programs and support networks for LGBTQ youth around the world. Recognizing the importance of guidance during pivotal moments of self-discovery, she has created safe spaces where young people can connect with mentors who have navigated similar journeys. These mentorship programs provide invaluable support, helping LGBTQ youth build resilience and empowering them to embrace their authentic selves.

3. **Promoting Mental Health and Well-being:** Nyla has been a vocal advocate for mental health and well-being within the LGBTQ community. She understands unique challenges faced by LGBTQ youth, such as societal rejection,

discrimination, and internalized homophobia or transphobia. Nyla has worked tirelessly to raise awareness about mental health issues and provide resources for young individuals struggling with their mental well-being. Through partnerships with mental health organizations and initiatives, she has made counseling and support services more accessible to LGBTQ youth.

4. **Campaigning for LGBTQ-Inclusive Education:** Nyla's influence extends to the education sector, where she has campaigned for LGBTQ-inclusive curriculum and safer school environments. Recognizing that education plays a fundamental role in shaping attitudes and perceptions, Nyla has worked with policymakers and educational institutions to introduce LGBTQ-inclusive materials, comprehensive sex education, and anti-bullying measures. By ensuring that LGBTQ youth see themselves reflected in their education, she has helped create more accepting and inclusive school environments.

5. **Advocacy for Legal Protections and Rights:** Nyla's advocacy work also extends to fighting for legal protections and rights for LGBTQ youth. She has actively campaigned and lobbied for the repeal of discriminatory laws and policies, advocating for equal rights in areas such as healthcare, housing, employment, and marriage. Nyla's high-profile court cases challenging discriminatory laws have set legal precedents and provided hope for LGBTQ youth around the world, inspiring them to fight for their own rights and equality.

6. **Promoting Positive Self-Image and Self-Acceptance:** Nyla constantly emphasizes the importance of self-love and self-acceptance for LGBTQ youth. Through her speeches and engagement on social media, she encourages young individuals to embrace their identities and find pride in who they are. Nyla champions body positivity and encourages LGBTQ youth to celebrate their uniqueness, challenging societal standards and fostering a sense of self-worth among young people who may have been marginalized or rejected.

7. **Empowering LGBTQ Youth Activism:** Perhaps one of the most significant ways Nyla influences LGBTQ youth is through empowering them to become activists and advocates themselves. By sharing her own journey and the impact she has made, she inspires young people to raise their voices and fight for change. Nyla provides tools, resources, and platforms for young activists, nurturing the next generation of LGBTQ advocates who will continue to push for equality and acceptance.

In conclusion, Nyla Ashen's influence on LGBTQ youth around the world is profound and far-reaching. Through her visibility, mentoring, advocacy, and empowerment, she has become a beacon of hope and resilience for countless young individuals. Nyla's unwavering commitment to equality and acceptance has helped shape a more inclusive world for LGBTQ youth, inspiring them to embrace their identities, fight for their rights, and believe in a brighter future.

importance of unconditional love and understanding. - Calls on the audience to embrace diversity and celebrate love beyond labels.

5. Inspiring Action: - Offers practical steps individuals can take to create a more inclusive society. - Encourages engagement with LGBTQ organizations and initiatives. - Calls on the audience to be allies and advocates for LGBTQ rights.

6. Conclusion: - Summarizes the key messages and takeaways from the talk. - Delivers a powerful closing statement that leaves a lasting impression on the audience. - Offers words of inspiration and hope for a future free from discrimination and prejudice.

Nyla Ashen's inspirational speeches and TED talks have become a catalyst for change, igniting conversations about LGBTQ rights and inspiring individuals around the world. Through her unique storytelling, data-driven approach, interactive presentations, and messages of resilience, Nyla continues to break down barriers and create a more accepting and inclusive society for all.

Nyla's Influence on LGBTQ Youth Around the World

Nyla Ashen's impact on LGBTQ youth around the world cannot be overstated. Through her advocacy work, inspiring speeches, and relatable presence in mainstream media, she has become a symbol of hope, empowerment, and resilience for countless young individuals struggling with their sexual orientation and gender identity.

1. **Fostering Representation and Visibility:** One of the key ways Nyla has influenced LGBTQ youth is by fostering representation and visibility. By being open about her own experiences and struggles, Nyla has shown young people that they are not alone. Through her media presence, Nyla has challenged stereotypes and showcased the diversity within the LGBTQ community. Her authenticity and unapologetic embrace of her identity have resonated with young individuals who often feel marginalized or invisible.

2. **Mentoring and Support:** Nyla has established mentoring programs and support networks for LGBTQ youth around the world. Recognizing the importance of guidance during pivotal moments of self-discovery, she has created safe spaces where young people can connect with mentors who have navigated similar journeys. These mentorship programs provide invaluable support, helping LGBTQ youth build resilience and empowering them to embrace their authentic selves.

3. **Promoting Mental Health and Well-being:** Nyla has been a vocal advocate for mental health and well-being within the LGBTQ community. She understands the unique challenges faced by LGBTQ youth, such as societal rejection,

discrimination, and internalized homophobia or transphobia. Nyla has worked tirelessly to raise awareness about mental health issues and provide resources for young individuals struggling with their mental well-being. Through partnerships with mental health organizations and initiatives, she has made counseling and support services more accessible to LGBTQ youth.

4. **Campaigning for LGBTQ-Inclusive Education:** Nyla's influence extends to the education sector, where she has campaigned for LGBTQ-inclusive curriculum and safer school environments. Recognizing that education plays a fundamental role in shaping attitudes and perceptions, Nyla has worked with policymakers and educational institutions to introduce LGBTQ-inclusive materials, comprehensive sex education, and anti-bullying measures. By ensuring that LGBTQ youth see themselves reflected in their education, she has helped create more accepting and inclusive school environments.

5. **Advocacy for Legal Protections and Rights:** Nyla's advocacy work also extends to fighting for legal protections and rights for LGBTQ youth. She has actively campaigned and lobbied for the repeal of discriminatory laws and policies, advocating for equal rights in areas such as healthcare, housing, employment, and marriage. Nyla's high-profile court cases challenging discriminatory laws have set legal precedents and provided hope for LGBTQ youth around the world, inspiring them to fight for their own rights and equality.

6. **Promoting Positive Self-Image and Self-Acceptance:** Nyla constantly emphasizes the importance of self-love and self-acceptance for LGBTQ youth. Through her speeches and engagement on social media, she encourages young individuals to embrace their identities and find pride in who they are. Nyla champions body positivity and encourages LGBTQ youth to celebrate their uniqueness, challenging societal standards and fostering a sense of self-worth among young people who may have been marginalized or rejected.

7. **Empowering LGBTQ Youth Activism:** Perhaps one of the most significant ways Nyla influences LGBTQ youth is through empowering them to become activists and advocates themselves. By sharing her own journey and the impact she has made, she inspires young people to raise their voices and fight for change. Nyla provides tools, resources, and platforms for young activists, nurturing the next generation of LGBTQ advocates who will continue to push for equality and acceptance.

In conclusion, Nyla Ashen's influence on LGBTQ youth around the world is profound and far-reaching. Through her visibility, mentoring, advocacy, and empowerment, she has become a beacon of hope and resilience for countless young individuals. Nyla's unwavering commitment to equality and acceptance has helped shape a more inclusive world for LGBTQ youth, inspiring them to embrace their identities, fight for their rights, and believe in a brighter future.

Chapter Three

Section One

Nyla's Fight for LGBTQ Rights in Qirona

In this section, we will delve into Nyla Ashen's relentless fight for LGBTQ rights in Qirona. Nyla recognized the discriminatory laws and policies that marginalized the LGBTQ community, and she made it her mission to challenge and change them. Her principled activism paved the way for significant progress and brought hope to countless individuals.

Challenging Discriminatory Laws and Policies

Nyla took an unyielding stance against the discriminatory laws and policies that targeted the LGBTQ community within Qirona. With a deep understanding of the legal system and a passion for justice, she fearlessly confronted these barriers head-on.

One of the most notable examples of Nyla's fight was her challenge against the archaic "Anti-Equality Act," a law that restricted LGBTQ individuals from accessing basic civil rights. Nyla rallied activists, legal experts, and community allies to highlight the inherent injustice of this legislation. Through public demonstrations, awareness campaigns, and strategic partnerships, Nyla successfully drew attention to the discriminatory nature of the act.

Nyla's Efforts in Promoting LGBTQ-Inclusive Education

Recognizing the power of education in shaping inclusive societies, Nyla focused on advocating for LGBTQ-inclusive education in Qirona. She firmly believed that by educating the next generation about diverse sexual orientations and gender identities, the cycle of discrimination could be broken.

Nyla collaborated with educational institutions, teachers, and students to develop LGBTQ-inclusive curricula and training programs. She conducted workshops and seminars, addressing misconceptions, fostering empathy, and promoting acceptance. Nyla's efforts in this domain not only empowered LGBTQ students to embrace their identities but also created a more inclusive environment for all.

The Impact of Nyla's Advocacy on the Legal System

Nyla's unwavering advocacy had a profound impact on the legal system in Qirona. Her relentless pursuit of justice resulted in landmark court cases that directly challenged discriminatory laws and set crucial precedents.

For instance, Nyla fought tirelessly for marriage equality, aiming to legalize same-sex marriages in Qirona. She employed a strategic legal approach, assembling a team of passionate lawyers and engaging with LGBTQ couples who yearned for their unions to be recognized. Drawing from international human rights conventions and constitutional principles, Nyla successfully argued for the fundamental right to marriage equality. The culmination of her efforts resulted in a groundbreaking court decision that legalized same-sex marriages in Qirona.

Nyla's Groundbreaking Court Cases

Throughout her activist journey, Nyla played a crucial role in several groundbreaking court cases that redefined LGBTQ rights in Qirona. One seminal case involved fighting against employment discrimination based on sexual orientation and gender identity. Nyla represented LGBTQ individuals who faced job loss and discrimination solely due to their identities. By challenging discriminatory practices, Nyla paved the way for legal protection and equality in the workplace.

In another landmark case, Nyla fought for transgender rights, centering on the recognition of gender identity and the right to self-determination. She advocated for the revision of identity documentation laws to ensure that transgender individuals could obtain accurate documents that aligned with their gender identity. Nyla's tenacity led to significant reforms, positively impacting the lives of countless transgender individuals who were previously marginalized and overlooked by the legal system.

An Unconventional Example: Nyla's "Power of Love" Campaign

One unconventional but effective campaign employed by Nyla was the "Power of Love" initiative. She recognized that changing hearts and minds was a crucial step towards achieving LGBTQ acceptance in Qirona. Nyla partnered with local artists, musicians, and influencers to create powerful and emotive pieces of art that promoted love, empathy, and understanding for the LGBTQ community.

Through this campaign, Nyla aimed to connect with individuals who may hold prejudiced views and help them recognize the humanity and worth of LGBTQ individuals. She organized interactive art exhibits, concerts, and performances that showcased the diverse experiences and stories of the LGBTQ community. By fostering empathy and challenging preconceived notions, Nyla's "Power of Love" campaign served as an influential force in driving societal change.

The Road Ahead: Continuing the Fight for Equality

While Nyla Ashen's fight for LGBTQ rights in Qirona brought about significant progress, her work is far from over. The battle for equality and acceptance is an ongoing one, and Nyla remains a beacon of inspiration for future generations.

To continue the fight, Nyla emphasizes the importance of alliances and partnerships within the LGBTQ community and beyond. Building bridges with other marginalized groups and working together towards common goals strengthens the collective voice for change.

Nyla also encourages continued education, awareness, and community engagement. By fostering dialogue, advocating for LGBTQ-inclusive policies, and amplifying marginalized voices, we can create a more inclusive society where every individual is treated with respect and dignity.

As Nyla's journey demonstrates, fighting for LGBTQ rights is not a solitary endeavor but a collective movement that requires perseverance, compassion, and relentless determination. Together, we can break down barriers, challenge discriminatory laws, and create a world where everyone—regardless of sexual orientation or gender identity—can thrive and live authentically.

Challenging discriminatory laws and policies

In the fight for LGBTQ rights, one of the crucial aspects is challenging discriminatory laws and policies that hinder equality and acceptance. Nyla Ashen, as a trailblazing LGBTQ activist, has devoted herself to dismantling these barriers in her home country of Qirona. With her tenacity and determination, Nyla has made significant strides in challenging discriminatory laws and policies. Let's delve into the strategies she employed and the impact she has had on Qirona's legal landscape.

Understanding the legal framework

Before Nyla could effectively challenge discriminatory laws and policies, she had to thoroughly understand the legal framework of Qirona and identify the specific areas that needed reform. With the help of legal experts, Nyla studied existing legislation that hindered LGBTQ rights.

One such discriminatory law was the "Marriage Act" that defined marriage as strictly between a man and a woman. Nyla recognized the need to advocate for marriage equality and worked tirelessly to challenge this law. She collaborated with LGBTQ organizations, legal scholars, and human rights activists to strategize the best approach.

Strategic litigation

Nyla employed strategic litigation as a powerful tool to challenge discriminatory laws and policies in Qirona. She filed strategic lawsuits against the government, arguing that these laws violated the principles of equality and non-discrimination.

For instance, in the landmark case of *Ashen v. Qirona*, Nyla argued that the existing "Marriage Act" infringed upon the rights of same-sex couples. She presented compelling legal arguments supported by extensive research and expert testimony to demonstrate that denying same-sex couples the right to marry was unconstitutional.

Nyla's strategic litigation not only aimed at changing laws but also at raising awareness and changing public opinion. She recognized the importance of using the legal system as a platform to educate society on the importance of LGBTQ equality and acceptance.

Engaging with lawmakers

Apart from strategic litigation, Nyla realized the significance of engaging with lawmakers to bring about legislative change. She actively lobbied members of parliament and met with key decision-makers to advocate for LGBTQ rights.

Nyla's approach involved sharing personal stories and experiences of LGBTQ individuals to humanize the issue and encourage empathy. She emphasized the need for comprehensive anti-discrimination laws that protect LGBTQ individuals in all aspects of life, including employment, housing, and public services.

By building relationships with lawmakers and gaining their support, Nyla played a critical role in shaping the discourse surrounding LGBTQ rights within the legislative chambers of Qirona.

Education and awareness campaigns

In addition to challenging discriminatory laws and policies through legal means, Nyla also recognized the importance of education and awareness campaigns to drive social change.

She spearheaded campaigns that aimed to debunk myths and dispel stereotypes about the LGBTQ community. Nyla collaborated with schools and educational institutions to implement LGBTQ-inclusive curriculum, promoting understanding and acceptance from an early age.

Nyla also utilized social media platforms to amplify her message and reach a broader audience. Through viral videos, informative graphics, and personal anecdotes, she sparked conversations and encouraged individuals to question their own biases and prejudices.

The role of international pressure

Nyla understood that challenging discriminatory laws and policies required not only domestic efforts but also international pressure. She strategically leveraged international human rights organizations and diplomatic channels to advocate for LGBTQ rights in Qirona.

By collaborating with renowned international organizations, Nyla was able to shed light on the human rights violations faced by LGBTQ individuals in her country. She called for the international community to exert pressure on the Qironan government to promote equality and protect the rights of all individuals, regardless of their sexual orientation or gender identity.

A lasting impact

Through her relentless efforts, Nyla Ashen has made remarkable progress in challenging discriminatory laws and policies in Qirona. The legal landscape pertaining to LGBTQ rights has significantly transformed, with the repeal or amendment of several discriminatory laws.

Nyla's advocacy has paved the way for marriage equality, comprehensive anti-discrimination laws, and increased societal acceptance of LGBTQ individuals. She has inspired a new generation of activists to continue the fight and has left an indelible mark on Qironan society.

However, Nyla recognizes that the fight for equality is an ongoing process. She remains optimistic and continues to work towards a future where LGBTQ individuals enjoy full equality and acceptance in Qirona and beyond.

Exercises

1. Research a case study from another country where strategic litigation was used to challenge discriminatory laws and policies. Analyze the specific legal strategies employed and the outcome of the case.

2. Organize an LGBTQ rights awareness campaign in your community. Utilize social media platforms, collaborate with local organizations, and educate others about the importance of equality and acceptance.

3. Write a persuasive letter to your local lawmaker advocating for comprehensive anti-discrimination laws that protect LGBTQ individuals. Highlight the importance of such legislation and the positive impact it can have on society as a whole.

Resources

- Human Rights Campaign: *LGBTQ Rights*
- International Lesbian, Gay, Bisexual, Trans and Intersex Association: *World Legal Wrap-Up*
- Amnesty International: *LGBTI Rights*
- TED Talk: Chimamanda Ngozi Adichie - *The Danger of a Single Story*

Remember, in the journey to challenge discriminatory laws and policies, every voice matters. Let Nyla Ashen's story inspire you to stand up, speak out, and fight for equality and acceptance. The path ahead may be challenging, but together, we can create a world where everyone is free to love and live authentically, regardless of their sexual orientation or gender identity.

Nyla's efforts in promoting LGBTQ-inclusive education

Nyla Ashen understood the power of education in shaping perceptions and creating a more inclusive society for LGBTQ individuals. In this section, we will explore her tireless efforts to promote LGBTQ-inclusive education in Qirona.

Understanding the importance of LGBTQ-inclusive education

Nyla recognized that education plays a vital role in challenging societal norms and promoting acceptance of LGBTQ individuals. She believed that by fostering safe and inclusive learning environments, students could develop empathy, understanding, and respect for people of all sexual orientations and gender identities.

Nyla's advocacy for LGBTQ-inclusive education stemmed from her own experiences of discrimination and exclusion within the educational system. She realized that it was crucial to create spaces where LGBTQ students could feel seen, valued, and supported.

Lobbying for policy changes

To achieve her goals, Nyla embarked on a campaign to advocate for policy changes that would integrate LGBTQ-inclusive curriculum and policies within schools across Qirona. She tirelessly met with education officials, lawmakers, and community leaders to raise awareness about the need for inclusive education.

Nyla's message was clear: LGBTQ-inclusive education would benefit not only LGBTQ students but also their peers and the entire school community. By teaching about diverse sexual orientations, gender identities, and LGBTQ history, schools could foster an environment of acceptance, reduce bullying, and create a more inclusive society.

Developing LGBTQ-inclusive curriculum

Nyla recognized the importance of developing LGBTQ-inclusive curriculum that would provide accurate and comprehensive information about LGBTQ issues. She collaborated with educators, LGBTQ activists, and scholars to create age-appropriate resources and materials for different grade levels.

The LGBTQ-inclusive curriculum emphasized the importance of respect, empathy, and inclusivity. It highlighted the achievements and contributions of LGBTQ individuals throughout history, showcasing their valuable role in shaping society. The curriculum also addressed common misconceptions and debunked stereotypes, helping students develop a more nuanced understanding of LGBTQ experiences.

Training educators and school staff

Recognizing that educators play a crucial role in creating LGBTQ-inclusive environments, Nyla spearheaded training programs for teachers and school staff. These programs focused on providing educators with the knowledge and tools to support LGBTQ students effectively.

The training sessions covered topics such as LGBTQ terminology, understanding gender identity, and strategies for creating safe spaces. Educators were also educated on the specific challenges faced by LGBTQ students and given guidance on how to address homophobia, transphobia, and other forms of discrimination in the classroom.

Creating support networks for LGBTQ students

In addition to advocating for LGBTQ-inclusive education, Nyla recognized the importance of providing support networks for LGBTQ students. She worked closely with LGBTQ organizations and student-led groups to establish safe spaces and mentorship programs within schools.

These support networks allowed LGBTQ students to connect with peers who shared similar experiences, providing a sense of belonging and support. Nyla organized events and workshops that celebrated LGBTQ identities and fostered a greater understanding of diverse sexual orientations and gender identities.

By promoting LGBTQ-inclusive education and creating support networks, Nyla Ashen left a lasting impact on Qirona's educational system. Through her efforts, more schools in Qirona began implementing inclusive policies and curricula, creating a more understanding and accepting society for generations to come.

A contemporary challenge: Addressing online LGBTQ bullying

While Nyla's efforts in promoting LGBTQ-inclusive education were commendable, she acknowledged that new challenges had emerged in the digital age. Online platforms had become breeding grounds for LGBTQ bullying and discrimination.

To address this issue, Nyla collaborated with technology companies and social media platforms to implement anti-bullying policies and tools specifically targeting LGBTQ-related harassment. She raised awareness about the harmful impacts of online bullying and encouraged students, educators, and parents to report incidents and seek support.

Nyla also organized workshops and seminars that focused on digital citizenship and responsible online behavior. These events aimed to empower LGBTQ students, teaching them how to navigate online spaces safely and minimize the harmful effects of online bullying.

Through her work in tackling online LGBTQ bullying, Nyla ensured that her advocacy extended beyond physical spaces and into the digital realm. By joining forces with technology companies and fostering digital resilience, she paved the way for safer online experiences for LGBTQ individuals.

Unconventional approach: LGBTQ storytelling events

One of Nyla's unconventional approaches to promoting LGBTQ-inclusive education was organizing LGBTQ storytelling events in schools. These events brought LGBTQ individuals from different walks of life to share their personal stories and experiences with students.

The LGBTQ storytelling events aimed to humanize the LGBTQ experience, challenge stereotypes, and foster empathy and understanding. By hearing firsthand narratives from LGBTQ individuals, students were able to develop a deeper appreciation for the challenges and triumphs of the LGBTQ community.

Nyla believed that storytelling had the power to create meaningful connections and break down barriers. The events not only educated students about LGBTQ identities but also empowered LGBTQ speakers, providing them with a platform to share their stories and be celebrated for their authenticity.

Resources for LGBTQ-inclusive education

To further support educators and schools in implementing LGBTQ-inclusive education, Nyla worked closely with LGBTQ organizations to develop and distribute resources. These resources included lesson plans, books, documentaries, and online materials that provided educators with the necessary tools to teach about LGBTQ issues effectively.

The resources also ensured that LGBTQ-inclusive education was not limited to one-off lessons but integrated seamlessly within various subjects and grade levels. They inspired critical thinking, fostered dialogue, and encouraged students to challenge discrimination and advocate for equality.

Nyla's collaboration with LGBTQ organizations and her efforts to develop resources for LGBTQ-inclusive education transformed the landscape of education in Qirona. Through her tireless work, she provided educators with the necessary support and tools to create inclusive learning environments that celebrate diversity and empower all students.

Conclusion

Nyla's efforts in promoting LGBTQ-inclusive education were instrumental in creating a more accepting and inclusive society in Qirona. By lobbying for policy changes, developing LGBTQ-inclusive curriculum, training educators, creating support networks, addressing online bullying, organizing storytelling events, and providing resources, she left a lasting impact on the education system.

Nyla's work laid the foundation for future generations of LGBTQ individuals to be seen, heard, and valued within the educational system. Her legacy serves as a reminder of the power of education in fostering empathy, understanding, and acceptance for all. As Qirona continues to strive for equality and inclusivity, Nyla Ashen's contributions will be celebrated and remembered as key milestones in the fight for LGBTQ rights.

The impact of Nyla's advocacy on the legal system

Nyla Ashen's unwavering dedication to LGBTQ rights in Qirona has had a profound impact on the legal system, challenging discriminatory laws and policies, and paving the way for greater equality and acceptance. Her relentless advocacy has not only brought about significant legal reforms but has also inspired a new generation of activists to fight for justice and equal rights.

1. Challenging discriminatory laws and policies:

Nyla Ashen's advocacy work has been instrumental in challenging and overturning discriminatory laws and policies that target the LGBTQ community in Qirona. Through strategic litigation and targeted campaigns, she has fought against laws that deny basic rights and freedoms to LGBTQ individuals. One such example is Nyla's successful challenge to the anti-gay "Conversion Therapy Act," which aimed to forcibly change a person's sexual orientation through harmful practices. Nyla's efforts resulted in the act being struck down as unconstitutional, highlighting the importance of protecting the rights of LGBTQ individuals.

2. Promoting LGBTQ-inclusive education:

Nyla Ashen recognizes the power of education in shaping societal attitudes towards the LGBTQ community. She has been a vocal advocate for LGBTQ-inclusive education, working closely with educational institutions and policymakers to integrate LGBTQ history, rights, and experiences into the curriculum. By promoting inclusive education, Nyla aims to foster empathy, understanding, and acceptance among students. Her efforts have resulted in the development of guidelines and programs that ensure LGBTQ students feel safe, valued, and represented within the education system.

3. Impact on the legal system:

Nyla Ashen's advocacy has had a ripple effect on the legal system, influencing lawmakers and judges to consider the rights and needs of the LGBTQ community. Her groundbreaking court cases have set important legal precedents, shaping future rulings and interpretations of LGBTQ rights. For instance, in the landmark case of Ashen v. Qirona, Nyla challenged discriminatory adoption laws that prohibited LGBTQ individuals from adopting children. The court ruled in her favor, declaring such laws unconstitutional and affirming the rights of LGBTQ individuals to become parents.

4. Empowering marginalized communities:

Nyla Ashen's advocacy goes beyond legal reforms; it empowers marginalized LGBTQ communities to assert their rights and demand justice. Through grassroots organizing and community engagement, she has encouraged marginalized individuals to come forward and share their experiences of discrimination, leading to increased public awareness and support for LGBTQ rights. Nyla's approach involves not only litigation but also grassroots movements, social media campaigns, and direct action to create lasting change in society.

5. Raising awareness through storytelling:

An unconventional yet highly effective aspect of Nyla Ashen's advocacy is her ability to humanize LGBTQ issues through storytelling. By sharing her personal experiences and those of other LGBTQ individuals, she has helped people understand the challenges and realities faced by the community. Nyla's storytelling approach has been instrumental in breaking down stereotypes and misconceptions, fostering empathy, and encouraging dialogue about LGBTQ rights. Her unique way of connecting with people through narratives has inspired countless individuals to reexamine their beliefs and support LGBTQ rights.

In conclusion, Nyla Ashen's advocacy has left an indelible mark on the legal system in Qirona. Through her tireless efforts, she has challenged discriminatory laws, promoted inclusive education, and empowered marginalized communities. Nyla's impact extends beyond legal reforms, as she has sparked a cultural shift by raising awareness and fostering empathy through storytelling. Her legacy serves as an inspiration for future generations of activists, reminding us of the power of advocacy in creating a more just and inclusive society.

Nyla's groundbreaking court cases

Nyla Ashen's relentless activism extended beyond public speaking and organizing rallies. She also took the fight for LGBTQ rights to the courtroom, using the power of law to challenge discriminatory practices and pave the way for equality and acceptance in Qirona. In this section, we will delve into some of Nyla's most groundbreaking court cases and explore their lasting impact on the LGBTQ community.

Case 1: Ashen v. Qirona Education Board

One of Nyla's earliest and most significant legal battles was against the Qirona Education Board. The board had consistently refused to include LGBTQ-inclusive curriculum in schools, denying students access to accurate information about sexual orientation and gender identities.

Nyla and her legal team argued that the Education Board's exclusionary policies violated students' right to inclusive education, perpetuating harmful stereotypes and contributing to the marginalization of LGBTQ youth. They presented extensive research and expert testimonies to demonstrate the positive impact of LGBTQ-inclusive education on mental health and overall well-being.

The court, recognizing the importance of providing an inclusive learning environment, ruled in Nyla's favor. As a result, the Qirona Education Board was required to revise its curriculum to include LGBTQ history, culture, and issues. This groundbreaking victory set a precedent for LGBTQ-inclusive education and sparked similar legal battles in other regions.

Case 2: Ashen v. Employment Discrimination

Nyla also fought for workplace equality, taking on cases of employment discrimination against LGBTQ individuals. In one significant case, she represented a transgender woman who had been unjustly terminated from her job based on her gender identity.

Nyla argued that the termination violated not only her client's rights but also undermined the principles of equal opportunity and fair treatment. She emphasized the importance of protecting transgender individuals from discrimination in the workplace and advocated for the implementation of comprehensive anti-discrimination policies.

The court ruled in favor of Nyla's client, acknowledging that discrimination based on gender identity constituted a violation of fundamental human rights. The decision brought attention to the need for stronger legal protections for LGBTQ employees and prompted discussions about legislative reforms to ensure equal opportunities for all.

Case 3: Ashen v. Marriage Equality

Nyla's fight for marriage equality was perhaps her most iconic court battle. In this landmark case, she challenged the constitutionality of Qirona's ban on same-sex marriage, arguing that it violated the principles of freedom, equality, and the right to happiness.

Nyla and her legal team presented compelling arguments, drawing upon case precedents, constitutional law, and sociological studies highlighting the positive effects of legalizing same-sex marriage. They demonstrated that denying LGBTQ individuals the right to marry perpetuated discrimination and denied them access to legal protections and benefits afforded to heterosexual couples.

After an intense legal battle that captivated the nation, the court struck down the ban on same-sex marriage, ruling it unconstitutional. Nyla's victory in this groundbreaking court case paved the way for LGBTQ couples to legally marry, granting them the same rights and recognition as their heterosexual counterparts.

Conclusion

Through her groundbreaking court cases, Nyla Ashen challenged discriminatory laws and policies, paving the way for LGBTQ equality in Qirona. Her victories in the courtroom not only brought about significant legal reforms but also inspired countless individuals to stand up for their rights.

Nyla's unwavering commitment to justice and equality continues to inspire the next generation of LGBTQ activists. As we celebrate her trailblazing journey, we must also recognize that the fight for LGBTQ rights is ongoing. Nyla's legacy reminds us that progress is possible through courage, perseverance, and the power of the law.

Section Two

Nyla's international recognition and accolades

Nyla Ashen's remarkable journey as an LGBTQ activist has garnered international recognition and numerous accolades. Her unwavering dedication to fighting for LGBTQ rights has propelled her to the forefront of the global movement. In this section, we will explore some of Nyla's most notable achievements and honors, highlighting the impact she has made on a global scale.

The Harvey Milk Medal of Honor

One of the most prestigious honors Nyla Ashen has received is the Harvey Milk Medal of Honor, named after the legendary LGBTQ rights activist, Harvey Milk. This esteemed award recognizes individuals who exhibit outstanding leadership and courage in advocating for LGBTQ rights. Nyla was presented with this medal for her unwavering commitment to equality, her groundbreaking activism, and her immense contributions to the LGBTQ community.

The Stonewall Award

In recognition of Nyla's extraordinary contributions to the fight for LGBTQ rights, she was bestowed with the highly esteemed Stonewall Award. Named after the iconic Stonewall riots of 1969, this award is given to those who have demonstrated exceptional bravery and perseverance in the face of adversity. Nyla's relentless efforts to challenge discriminatory laws, promote inclusivity, and provoke positive change made her a deserving recipient of this prestigious accolade.

The Queer Champion Award

As her influence and impact continued to grow, Nyla Ashen was honored with the Queer Champion Award. This award celebrates individuals who have shown exemplary dedication in advancing LGBTQ rights and creating a more inclusive society. Nyla's relentless advocacy work, combined with her ability to captivate and inspire audiences, has solidified her status as a trailblazer and role model within the LGBTQ community.

Time Magazine's 100 Most Influential People

Nyla's remarkable achievements and impact have not gone unnoticed by the international media. Time Magazine recognized her as one of the 100 Most

SECTION TWO 69

Influential People in the world, acknowledging her significant role in shaping public opinion and challenging societal norms. This recognition showcased Nyla's ability to not only advocate for LGBTQ rights but also to inspire change on a global scale.

UNESCO Equality Champion

Nyla Ashen's contributions to the LGBTQ community extend far beyond national borders. Her dedication to promoting equality and acceptance prompted UNESCO to appoint her as an Equality Champion. In this role, she actively works alongside global LGBTQ advocates to develop strategies and initiatives that prioritize the well-being and rights of LGBTQ individuals worldwide. Nyla's involvement with UNESCO further solidifies her status as a global leader in the fight for LGBTQ rights.

The Nyla Ashen Scholarship Fund

In addition to the various awards and accolades she has received, Nyla Ashen has established the Nyla Ashen Scholarship Fund. This fund aims to provide financial assistance to LGBTQ youth pursuing higher education or vocational training. By empowering young LGBTQ individuals to pursue their dreams, Nyla seeks to create a more inclusive and equitable world for future generations.

Nyla Ashen's international recognition and accolades serve as a testament to her unwavering determination, remarkable leadership, and relentless advocacy. Her impact on the global LGBTQ rights movement cannot be understated, and her legacy will continue to inspire and empower LGBTQ individuals for generations to come.

Note: Nyla's journey is an inspiration to all, and her achievements remind us of the importance of standing up for what we believe in. While Nyla has achieved great success, it is essential to recognize that there is still much work to be done in the fight for LGBTQ rights. Let Nyla's story serve as a call to action, motivating each one of us to contribute to a world where equality and acceptance reign.

Awards and honors for Nyla's activism

Nyla Ashen's relentless dedication to LGBTQ activism has not only transformed lives but also earned her numerous prestigious awards and honors. Her groundbreaking work in challenging discriminatory laws, promoting LGBTQ rights, and empowering marginalized communities has garnered recognition and accolades from various organizations and institutions worldwide. In this section, we will delve into some of the remarkable awards and honors bestowed upon Nyla for her exceptional activism.

Champion of Equality Award

One of the most notable honors Nyla received for her contributions to LGBTQ activism is the esteemed Champion of Equality Award. This award, presented annually by the International LGBTQ Rights Organization (ILR), recognizes individuals who have made a significant impact on advancing LGBTQ rights and advocating for equality. Nyla was a recipient of this prestigious award in recognition of her tireless efforts in fighting for equal rights, challenging discriminatory policies, and amplifying the voices of the marginalized.

Humanitarian of the Year

Nyla's unwavering commitment to creating a more inclusive society and improving the well-being of LGBTQ individuals earned her the prestigious title of Humanitarian of the Year. This honor, bestowed by the LGBTQ Empowerment Foundation, celebrates individuals who have shown extraordinary compassion, leadership, and dedication to uplifting vulnerable communities. Nyla's passion for equality, her inspiring advocacy, and her ability to effect positive change in the lives of many made her a deserving recipient of this esteemed award.

Global Activism Award

In recognition of her global impact on LGBTQ activism, Nyla Ashen was honored with the Global Activism Award by the United Nations Human Rights Council. This award celebrates individuals who have transcended borders and made a significant difference in the fight for human rights and equality. Nyla's resolute efforts to challenge discriminatory laws, advance LGBTQ rights, and amplify marginalized voices around the world exemplify the spirit of this prestigious award.

Advocate of the Year

Another notable accolade that Nyla Ashen earned for her remarkable advocacy work is the Advocate of the Year award. Presented by the LGBTQ Advocacy Alliance, this honor highlights the exceptional efforts of individuals who have made significant contributions to advancing LGBTQ rights and empowering the community. Nyla's ability to mobilize support, foster dialogue, and create lasting change through her advocacy made her an outstanding recipient of this prestigious award.

Trailblazer Award

Nyla Ashen's unparalleled determination, resilience, and ability to break boundaries earned her the Trailblazer Award from the LGBTQ Action Network. This award recognizes individuals who have pioneered new paths, challenged societal norms, and created opportunities for the LGBTQ community. Nyla's groundbreaking activism, innovative approach, and significant impact in promoting equality and acceptance contributed to her deserving recognition as a Trailblazer.

Inclusive Education Champion

Nyla Ashen's dedication to promoting LGBTQ-inclusive education and creating safer spaces for LGBTQ youth earned her the title of Inclusive Education Champion. Presented by the National Organization for LGBTQ Education, this award acknowledges individuals who have shown exceptional leadership and advocacy in promoting inclusive educational practices. Nyla's tireless efforts to challenge discriminatory policies, train educators, and advocate for LGBTQ-inclusive curricula made her an outstanding recipient of this honorable award.

Trickster's Award

In addition to more traditional accolades, Nyla Ashen's ability to challenge societal expectations and use humor to combat discrimination earned her the distinguished Trickster's Award from the LGBTQ Humor Society. This award celebrated Nyla's creative use of wit and levity to bring attention to serious LGBTQ issues in a refreshing and engaging way. Nyla's ability to blend activism with humor and capture the hearts of many made her a worthy recipient of this unconventional yet significant award.

Unconventional Activism Prize

Nyla Ashen's innovative approach to LGBTQ advocacy and her ability to create impactful change through unconventional means earned her the Unconventional Activism Prize. Presented by the LGBTQ Coalition for Creative Advocacy, this award reflects Nyla's ability to challenge traditional norms, think outside the box, and create new avenues for change. Nyla's creative projects, such as harnessing the power of social media and collaborating with LGBTQ influencers, exemplify the spirit of this esteemed award.

Conclusion

Nyla Ashen's tireless efforts, passion, and determination have earned her numerous awards and honors for her exceptional LGBTQ activism. From global recognition for her impact on human rights to unconventional awards celebrating her creative approach, Nyla's trailblazing journey continues to inspire future generations of LGBTQ activists. Through her unwavering dedication and innovative strategies, Nyla has left an indelible mark on the fight for equality and acceptance, paving the way for a future where LGBTQ individuals can thrive without fear of discrimination or prejudice.

As we embark on the next chapter of Nyla Ashen's journey, let us remember the importance of recognizing and celebrating those who challenge societal norms, fight for justice, and empower marginalized communities. In the face of adversity, Nyla's remarkable accomplishments remind us that change is possible, and together, we can build a world that values and respects the rights and dignity of every individual.

Nyla's keynote speeches at LGBTQ conferences worldwide

Nyla Ashen's impactful presence in the LGBTQ community extended far beyond her activism in Qirona. Her keynote speeches at LGBTQ conferences worldwide became a platform for her to share her experiences, insights, and strategies for promoting equality and acceptance. Nyla's ability to connect with her audience and inspire change made her a highly sought-after speaker at these influential gatherings.

The Power of Sharing Personal Stories

Nyla's keynote speeches were centered around the power of storytelling. She emphasized the importance of individuals sharing their personal stories to create empathy and understanding among a wider audience. Nyla believed that by sharing their experiences, LGBTQ individuals could humanize their struggles and build bridges of compassion.

During her speeches, Nyla would recount her own journey of self-discovery and the challenges she had faced as a queer person. By sharing her vulnerabilities, she aimed to inspire others to embrace their true selves and fight for their rights passionately. Nyla's ability to weave her personal narrative into her speeches created an emotional connection with her listeners, ensuring that her message resonated on a deeper level.

Addressing the Intersectionality of LGBTQ Issues

Nyla recognized that LGBTQ individuals are not a monolithic group and that their experiences are shaped by other identities they hold, such as race, ethnicity, and socioeconomic background. In her keynote speeches, she focused on the intersectionality of LGBTQ issues and demonstrated the necessity of considering the unique struggles faced by different communities within the larger LGBTQ movement.

By highlighting the experiences of marginalized LGBTQ groups, Nyla aimed to foster inclusivity and solidarity within the community. She urged her audience to recognize their privilege and actively work towards dismantling systems of oppression that perpetuate discrimination and inequality. Nyla's speeches sparked conversations and inspired action to create a more diverse and inclusive LGBTQ movement.

Using Data and Research to Advocate for Change

Nyla firmly believed that data and research could be powerful tools in advocating for LGBTQ rights. In her keynote speeches, she presented compelling statistics and studies that highlighted the disparities and challenges faced by the LGBTQ community. By grounding her arguments in data, she aimed to dispel misconceptions and encourage evidence-based decision-making.

Nyla also shared success stories and examples of LGBTQ-inclusive policies and practices from around the world. She stressed the importance of highlighting these positive changes to inspire and guide further progress in other regions. Nyla's use of research and data provided her audience with tangible evidence of the positive impact that activism and advocacy can have on LGBTQ rights.

Interactive Workshops and Skill-building Sessions

In addition to delivering keynote speeches, Nyla also hosted interactive workshops and skill-building sessions at LGBTQ conferences. These sessions provided practical tools, strategies, and resources for activists and allies to create change within their communities.

Nyla facilitated discussions on grassroots organizing, effective communication strategies, and community mobilization. She encouraged individuals to explore their unique strengths and find avenues where they could contribute meaningfully to the LGBTQ movement. These workshops not only empowered attendees with valuable skills but also fostered a sense of community and collaboration.

Unconventional Approach: The Power of Performance

One unconventional aspect of Nyla's keynote speeches was her incorporation of performance art. Recognizing the impact of creative expression, she integrated elements of spoken word poetry, music, and dance into her presentations. Nyla believed that art had the power to evoke emotions and inspire change in ways that traditional speeches sometimes couldn't.

Through her performances, Nyla aimed to create a multisensory experience for her audience. She used her creative talents to tell stories, convey messages of resilience, and provoke thought. Nyla's unique approach captivated her listeners and left a lasting impression, effectively engaging them in the pursuit of LGBTQ equality.

Overall, Nyla Ashen's keynote speeches at LGBTQ conferences worldwide were a testament to her exceptional ability to inspire, educate, and mobilize. Through personal storytelling, an intersectional approach, data-driven advocacy, interactive workshops, and unconventional performance, Nyla left an indelible mark on the global LGBTQ community, fueling the ongoing fight for equality and acceptance.

The global impact of Nyla's activism

Nyla Ashen's activism has had a profound global impact, inspiring and empowering LGBTQ individuals all over the world. Her relentless advocacy has pushed for change, sparked conversations, and paved the way for a more inclusive and accepting society. In this section, we will explore the various ways in which Nyla's activism has made a difference on a global scale.

Change in Legislation

Nyla's fight for LGBTQ rights has extended far beyond the borders of Qirona. Her relentless efforts have challenged discriminatory laws and policies in countries worldwide, where homosexuality is still criminalized. Through her global network of allies and advocacy organizations, Nyla has strategically collaborated with local activists to bring about legal reforms.

One remarkable example is Nyla's involvement in decriminalizing homosexuality in Elysia, a country where same-sex relationships were punishable by law. Nyla's passionate speeches and collaboration with local LGBTQ activists shed light on the injustices faced by the community. Her tireless efforts resulted in a groundbreaking court case that ultimately led to the repeal of the anti-LGBTQ legislation, setting a precedent for change in other parts of the world.

Promoting LGBTQ-Inclusive Education

Education plays a fundamental role in breaking down stereotypes, fostering understanding, and creating a more tolerant society. Nyla has recognized the significance of LGBTQ-inclusive education and its impact on shaping the minds of future generations.

Through partnerships with educational institutions, Nyla has spearheaded initiatives to incorporate LGBTQ history, experiences, and contributions into school curricula. By highlighting the achievements of LGBTQ individuals throughout history, Nyla's activism has instilled pride and empowered LGBTQ youth to embrace their authentic selves.

Nyla has also actively advocated for safer and more inclusive school environments, where LGBTQ students are protected from bullying and discrimination. Her advocacy for inclusive policies and support systems has helped create spaces where LGBTQ youth feel accepted and empowered to excel academically and socially.

Global Visibility and Representation

Nyla's reach and influence have transcended borders, thanks to her impactful presence in mainstream media. By seizing opportunities to appear on TV interviews, talk shows, and news segments, Nyla has used her platform to amplify the voices of LGBTQ individuals and shed light on the issues they face.

Her viral social media moments have captivated audiences around the world, increasing awareness of LGBTQ rights and fostering conversations about acceptance. Whether it's through heartfelt personal stories, humorous anecdotes, or thought-provoking discussions, Nyla has effectively engaged people from all walks of life, encouraging empathy and understanding.

Furthermore, Nyla's collaboration with prominent LGBTQ influencers has expanded her reach and brought attention to LGBTQ issues on a global scale. By working together with individuals who have large online followings, Nyla has been able to mobilize support, raise funds for LGBTQ organizations, and amplify her advocacy efforts.

Symbol of Hope and Resilience

Nyla's unwavering dedication to LGBTQ rights has made her a symbol of hope and resilience for millions of individuals around the world. Her courage in the face of adversity has inspired countless LGBTQ youth to embrace their true selves and believe in a better future.

Nyla's keynote speeches at LGBTQ conferences worldwide have provided a platform for sharing her experiences, strategies, and insights. These speeches have not only motivated activists but also educated others about the ongoing struggles faced by the LGBTQ community. Nyla's ability to connect with her audience, infused with her trademark wit and charm, leaves a lasting impact on everyone she addresses.

Beyond her activism, Nyla's personal struggles and triumphs have made her relatable and approachable to LGBTQ individuals worldwide. Her openness about mental health challenges and self-care resonates with many who face similar struggles. By sharing her own journey, Nyla offers guidance and support, emphasizing the importance of holistic well-being in the midst of fighting for a better world.

Celebrating Diversity and Unity

One of the most significant contributions of Nyla's activism is her emphasis on the celebration of diversity within the LGBTQ community. Through her speeches, media presence, and collaborations, Nyla has encouraged inclusivity and unity among different LGBTQ identities and experiences.

Nyla recognizes that the fight for LGBTQ rights is not a one-size-fits-all approach. She actively supports intersectional perspectives, acknowledging the unique challenges faced by LGBTQ individuals of color, transgender individuals, and those from economically disadvantaged backgrounds. By amplifying diverse voices and experiences, Nyla fosters a sense of belonging within the LGBTQ community, ensuring that no one is left behind.

In conclusion, Nyla Ashen's activism has had an undeniable global impact. Through her tireless efforts in challenging discriminatory laws, promoting LGBTQ-inclusive education, increasing global visibility and representation, inspiring others as a symbol of hope and resilience, and celebrating diversity and unity, Nyla has left an indelible mark on the world. Her legacy will continue to shape the fight for LGBTQ rights, inspiring future generations to advocate for a more inclusive and accepting world.

Nyla's role as a symbol of hope and resilience

Nyla Ashen's unwavering dedication to her activism has made her a symbol of hope and resilience for the LGBTQ community worldwide. Through her tireless efforts, Nyla has become a beacon of light, inspiring others to stand up for their rights and fight against discrimination. In this section, we will explore the various ways in which Nyla embodies hope and resilience, and how her influence continues to impact the lives of LGBTQ individuals.

Embracing Identity and Overcoming Adversity

Nyla's journey of self-discovery and embracing her true identity serves as an inspiration to countless individuals facing similar struggles. Growing up in a society that often shunned LGBTQ individuals, Nyla faced discrimination and adversity from a young age. However, she never allowed these challenges to define her, but rather used them as fuel to ignite change.

By openly embracing her identity and sharing her story, Nyla has shown that it is possible to rise above societal pressures and be proud of who you are. She has become a role model for LGBTQ individuals who may still be afraid to embrace their true selves, offering them hope that they too can find acceptance and live authentically.

Leading by Example

Nyla's resilience and determination in the face of opposition have made her a powerful leader in the LGBTQ community. She fearlessly takes on discriminatory policies and challenges the status quo, reminding others that change is possible. Nyla's unwavering commitment to her cause serves as a powerful example for LGBTQ activists around the world.

Through her activism, Nyla demonstrates that individuals have the power to effect change, no matter how daunting the obstacles may seem. Her ability to rally support and engage allies in her fight is a testament to her leadership skills and charisma. Nyla's inclusive and empowering approach has not only brought about tangible change but also inspired others to take action in their own communities.

Building a Supportive Community

One of the most remarkable aspects of Nyla's journey is her dedication to building a supportive and inclusive community for LGBTQ individuals. Recognizing the importance of allyship, Nyla has actively worked to foster connections and unite people from diverse backgrounds.

Through LGBTQ organizations and her advocacy work, Nyla has created safe spaces for people to come together, share their experiences, and support one another. By providing platforms for dialogue and education, she has helped to break down barriers and foster understanding among different communities.

Nyla's ability to connect with people on a personal level has allowed her to inspire hope and resilience in both LGBTQ individuals and allies. Her impact goes beyond her own achievements, as she encourages others to join the fight for equality and acceptance.

Spreading Positivity and Empowerment

In addition to her activism, Nyla has become known for her infectious positivity and empowering messages. She uses her platform to promote self-love and acceptance, encouraging individuals to embrace their uniqueness and celebrate their identities.

Through her social media presence and public speaking engagements, Nyla shares uplifting stories and personal anecdotes, inspiring her audience to persevere and believe in themselves. Her words of encouragement resonate with LGBTQ youth who may be struggling with their own identities or facing adversity.

Nyla's ability to inspire hope through her words and actions showcases her resilience and unwavering spirit. She reminds us all that even in the face of adversity, there is always hope for a brighter future.

Conclusion: Continuing the Legacy

Nyla Ashen's role as a symbol of hope and resilience extends far beyond her own achievements. Her unwavering dedication to LGBTQ rights and equality has inspired countless individuals to stand up for their rights and fight against discrimination.

As Nyla's impact continues to ripple through societies, her legacy serves as a reminder that hope and resilience are essential in the battle for equality. By remaining steadfast in the face of adversity and embracing our true selves, we can create a world where all LGBTQ individuals are seen, heard, and accepted.

Nyla's journey is a testament to the power of one individual's unwavering commitment to making a difference. Her resilience in the face of opposition and her ability to inspire hope have left an indelible mark on the LGBTQ community and will continue to shape the fight for equality for generations to come.

Section Three

Nyla's personal struggles and triumphs

Nyla Ashen's journey as an LGBTQ activist has been filled with both remarkable triumphs and personal struggles. In this section, we will explore the challenges she faced and the triumphs she achieved on her path to becoming a trailblazer and symbol of hope for the LGBTQ community.

Navigating relationships and love as an LGBTQ activist

Love and relationships are aspects of life that everyone desires, regardless of their sexual orientation or gender identity. For Nyla Ashen, being an LGBTQ activist added an extra layer of complexity to her personal life. As she fought for LGBTQ rights and equality, she also had to navigate her own journey in finding love and maintaining healthy relationships.

Nyla's personal struggles in this area were twofold. Firstly, she faced the challenge of finding partners who fully understood and supported her activism. Nyla desired a partner who could share her passion for advocacy and be by her side through the ups and downs of her activism journey. However, she often found it difficult to find individuals who could handle the demands and emotional toll that being an activist entailed.

Secondly, Nyla faced the challenge of coming out to potential partners and their families. The fear of rejection and discrimination loomed over her, as she wondered if her activism would be seen as a threat or if her potential partner's family would struggle to accept her. The emotional weight of this added pressure took a toll on Nyla's mental health, as she grappled with the fear of vulnerability and the potential consequences of being open about her identity.

Despite these challenges, Nyla received unwavering support and love from the LGBTQ community. Through networking and LGBTQ events, she met individuals who understood the intricacies of activism and were willing to support her on her journey. These relationships not only brought Nyla comfort and joy, but they also served as a constant reminder of the resilience and strength of the LGBTQ community.

Coming out to her family and community

One of the most significant personal struggles Nyla faced was coming out to her family and community. The fear of rejection and the uncertainty of how her loved ones would react weighed heavily on her heart. Nyla knew that her coming out would not only impact her personal relationships but also influence her activism.

With trepidation and courage, Nyla decided to share her truth with her family and close friends. She prepared herself for a range of reactions, from acceptance and support to confusion and even rejection. The process was emotionally exhausting, as Nyla grappled with the fear of losing those she held dear in her life.

However, Nyla was met with an outpouring of love and support from her family and friends. They embraced her wholeheartedly, recognizing the importance of living an authentic life and standing proudly in her identity. This acceptance became a source of strength for Nyla as she continued her activism work, knowing that she had a strong foundation of love and support behind her.

Furthermore, Nyla's coming-out journey had a profound impact on her community. By sharing her story, she challenged stereotypes and offered hope to those who were still struggling to come to terms with their own identities. Nyla's vulnerability and authenticity inspired countless individuals to embrace their true selves, empowering them to live openly and authentically.

Nyla's reflections on mental health and self-care

Balancing the demands of activism with personal well-being is a challenge that many activists face. Nyla Ashen was no exception. Throughout her journey, she learned the importance of prioritizing her mental health and practicing self-care.

As Nyla faced the relentless discrimination and backlash that often accompanied her activism, she experienced periods of emotional strain and burnout. The weight of fighting for equal rights while facing opposition and hatred took a toll on her well-being. To overcome these challenges, Nyla turned to various strategies to nurture her mental health.

One of the key aspects of Nyla's self-care routine was seeking support from therapists and counselors who specialized in working with LGBTQ individuals. These professionals provided her with a safe space to process her emotions, explore coping mechanisms, and develop resilience in the face of adversity.

Moreover, Nyla found solace in engaging in activities that brought her joy and allowed her to disconnect from the stresses of activism. Whether it was indulging in her favorite hobbies, spending time in nature, or simply taking a break from social media, these moments of respite provided her with the energy and clarity needed to continue her fight for LGBTQ rights.

Nyla's reflections on mental health and self-care serve as a reminder that activism is a marathon, not a sprint. Taking care of oneself is essential to sustaining the energy and passion required to create lasting change.

Finding balance between activism and personal life

Achieving a balance between her activism and personal life was an ongoing challenge for Nyla. The intense focus and dedication required to fight for LGBTQ rights often meant sacrificing personal time and relationships. Nyla became acutely aware of the need to find a harmonious equilibrium between her passion for activism and the other aspects of her life.

To address this challenge, Nyla developed strategies that allowed her to maintain a sense of balance. She implemented strict boundaries around her work hours, ensuring that she had dedicated time for self-care, relationships, and personal pursuits. Nyla recognized that without a well-rounded life, her activism would become unsustainable, and she would be unable to serve as a beacon of hope for others.

Additionally, Nyla emphasized the importance of building a strong support system. Surrounding herself with individuals who understood the demands of activism and prioritized her well-being played a crucial role in maintaining balance. These individuals not only provided emotional support, but they also encouraged Nyla to take breaks, recharge, and celebrate her personal milestones.

In finding this delicate balance, Nyla's personal life flourished alongside her activism. She forged meaningful connections, experienced personal growth, and developed resilience in the face of challenges. This balance became one of the key factors that contributed to her ability to create a lasting impact on LGBTQ rights in Qirona and beyond.

Unconventional but Relevant Example: The Power of Vulnerability

A powerful example of Nyla's personal struggle and triumph was her TED talk titled "The Power of Vulnerability." In this unforgettable speech, Nyla courageously shared her journey as an LGBTQ activist, highlighting the challenges she had faced and the triumphs she had achieved.

Instead of presenting a polished narrative of her success, Nyla chose to embrace vulnerability and share the unfiltered reality of her experiences. Through raw honesty and personal anecdotes, she captivated the audience, allowing them to connect with her on a deeply emotional level.

By sharing her personal struggles and triumphs, Nyla broke down barriers and shattered stereotypes surrounding LGBTQ individuals and activism. She showed that being true to oneself and embracing vulnerability can lead to empowerment and inspire change.

Nyla's TED talk became a viral sensation, reaching millions around the world. It resonated deeply with individuals who had faced discrimination, struggled with their identity, or aspired to fight for a cause they believed in. The talk became a catalyst for conversations about LGBTQ rights, acceptance, and the power of personal narratives in driving social change.

This example demonstrates the unconventional yet deeply relevant impact of Nyla's personal struggles and triumphs. It serves as a reminder of the power of vulnerability in sparking empathy, driving conversations, and inspiring individuals to take action.

Conclusion

In this section, we explored Nyla Ashen's personal struggles and triumphs as an LGBTQ activist. From navigating relationships and coming out to her family and community, to prioritizing mental health and finding balance between activism and personal life, Nyla's journey was filled with challenges and growth.

Nyla's personal struggles and triumphs are a testament to the resilience and courage of LGBTQ activists. Her unwavering dedication to creating a more inclusive and accepting society has left an indelible mark on the LGBTQ community in Qirona and beyond.

As we conclude this section, let us celebrate Nyla's trailblazing journey, recognizing the lasting impact she has made on LGBTQ rights, and draw inspiration from her words of wisdom. The fight for equality and acceptance continues, and Nyla's legacy serves as a guiding light for the next generation of LGBTQ activists and advocates.

Navigating relationships and love as an LGBTQ activist

Love is a beautiful and complex journey, filled with joy, challenges, and growth. For LGBTQ activists like Nyla Ashen, the path to love can be even more intricate. In this section, we will explore the unique experiences and obstacles Nyla faced while navigating relationships and love as an LGBTQ activist. We will delve into the intersections of love, activism, and personal growth, highlighting the importance of self-acceptance, support, and communication.

As an LGBTQ activist, Nyla had a deep understanding of the power relationships hold in promoting positive change. She recognized that for society to truly embrace LGBTQ rights, it was essential for individuals to see loving, healthy same-sex relationships. Nyla's own experiences in love became a testament to the fact that love knows no boundaries and that LGBTQ relationships are just as valid and meaningful as any other.

However, being in the public eye as an activist meant that Nyla's relationships faced scrutiny and speculation. Rumors and controversies often surrounded her personal life, adding an extra layer of pressure and complexity. Nyla's resilience and unwavering dedication to her cause helped her navigate through these challenges, staying true to herself and her partners.

One key aspect that Nyla emphasized was the importance of self-acceptance in finding love and maintaining healthy relationships. For her, embracing her true identity and loving herself unconditionally were the foundations on which she built her romantic connections. Nyla believed that only by accepting ourselves, flaws, and all, can we truly give and receive love.

Communication played a vital role in Nyla's relationships. Open and honest conversations about her activism, struggles, and achievements helped establish a strong foundation of understanding and support. Nyla's partners admired her passion and dedication, but also acknowledged the toll it could take on her emotionally. They formed a support system that embraced her activism and offered a safe space for her to be vulnerable and recharge.

Navigating relationships as an LGBTQ activist also meant grappling with societal expectations and cultural norms. Nyla understood the importance of challenging and redefining these norms, paving the way for love to flourish in all its forms. Her relationships served as a source of inspiration, proving that love defies societal constraints and has the power to transform hearts and minds.

Nyla's journey taught her that finding love as an LGBTQ activist is not without its hurdles. It requires resilience, understanding, and a commitment to growth. But it also offers immense joy and the opportunity to be part of a love story that transcends boundaries and helps shape a more inclusive society.

Example Problem: Navigating Intimacy in a Public Space

Imagine you are an LGBTQ activist attending a pride parade with your partner. The event is crowded, and you both are overcome with emotions of love, pride, and activism. However, you start feeling uncomfortable expressing your affection due to the fear of judgment or potential backlash.

1. How can you navigate this situation and maintain a healthy demonstration of love while being mindful of your surroundings?

Solution: It is essential to prioritize safety and comfort in such public spaces. Talk openly with your partner about your concerns and find a compromise that feels right for both of you. This could involve holding hands, discreet gestures of affection, or finding queer-friendly spaces where you can freely express your love without worries.

Remember that love is an act of resistance, and every small act of affection can help challenge societal norms and pave the way for acceptance and inclusivity. Be proud of your relationship and take inspiration from LGBTQ activists like Nyla Ashen, who fearlessly embraced love and fought for equality.

Additional Resources: - "The Velvet Rage: Overcoming the Pain of Growing Up Gay in a Straight Man's World" by Alan Downs - "This Book is Gay" by Juno Dawson - "Love, Simon" (2018), a film depicting the challenges and joys of

LGBTQ love - LGBTQ-inclusive therapy and support groups in your local community - Online LGBTQ activist communities and discussion forums

Coming out to her family and community

Coming out is a deeply personal and courageous journey that many LGBTQ individuals experience. Nyla Ashen's story of coming out to her family and community is an important part of her trailblazing journey as an LGBTQ activist. In this section, we will explore Nyla's experiences, the challenges she faced, and the impact her coming out had on her personal and professional life.

Navigating the complexities of family dynamics

Coming out to one's family can be daunting, especially when faced with the fear of rejection or misunderstanding. For Nyla, this process was both liberating and challenging. With her unconventional upbringing, Nyla had learned to embrace her true self and identify as a member of the LGBTQ community.

However, she knew that not everyone in her family would immediately understand or accept her identity. She carefully considered the right time and approach to have this conversation, ensuring that she would be supported and loved throughout the journey.

Nyla's coming-out experience varied among her family members. Some embraced her identity with open arms, showering her with love and support. Others needed time to process the information and understand what it meant for Nyla. In some cases, Nyla had to engage in difficult conversations, educating her family about LGBTQ experiences, dispelling myths and misconceptions, and fostering understanding and acceptance.

Embracing her community with pride

Coming out to the broader community can be a transformative experience for an LGBTQ individual. It requires courage and resilience, as one risks facing discrimination and prejudice. Nyla Ashen's journey was no different.

When Nyla decided to come out to her community, she understood the importance of being a visible and authentic advocate. By sharing her own story, she hoped to inspire others and create a safe space for dialogue and acceptance. Nyla believed that visibility leads to education, and education leads to acceptance.

She began by engaging in local LGBTQ organizations and events, connecting with others who shared similar experiences. Through these connections, Nyla found strength and support in a community of like-minded individuals who understood the challenges she faced. Together, they created a network of support and empowerment.

With this newfound support, Nyla started participating in pride parades and LGBTQ awareness campaigns. She spoke at community events, sharing her personal journey with vulnerability and authenticity. As an LGBTQ activist, Nyla aimed to challenge stereotypes, break down barriers, and promote understanding and acceptance in her community.

Overcoming challenges and finding acceptance

Nyla encountered various challenges on her journey of coming out to her family and community. She faced instances of discrimination, ignorance, and even hostility. However, she refused to let these obstacles deter her from her mission.

Nyla's determination and resilience helped her navigate through difficult conversations and confrontations. She used her platform as an activist to educate others, promoting empathy, and fostering dialogue. Nyla firmly believed that change begins with understanding, and she dedicated herself to creating positive change.

Through her advocacy work and personal stories, Nyla touched the lives of many, offering support and inspiration to those who were also on their own coming-out journey. Her messages of self-acceptance, love, and resilience resonated with both LGBTQ individuals and allies, empowering them to embrace their identities and support others in their journey.

Resources and support for individuals coming out

Coming out can be an overwhelming and emotional experience, and it is crucial for individuals to have access to resources and support during this time. Nyla Ashen recognized the importance of providing assistance to those going through the coming-out process.

She collaborated with LGBTQ organizations to develop resources such as helplines, support groups, and online forums. These resources offered guidance, emotional support, and a safe space for individuals to share their stories and seek advice.

Additionally, Nyla worked alongside mental health professionals to address the unique challenges faced by LGBTQ individuals during the coming-out process. She advocated for inclusive counseling services that catered to the specific needs of the community, ensuring that mental health support was readily available.

Embracing individuality and celebrating diversity

Nyla Ashen's coming-out journey was not just about her personal experience; it was a representation of the countless LGBTQ individuals who yearn for acceptance and understanding.

Through her own journey, Nyla aimed to break down societal barriers and reshape perceptions surrounding LGBTQ identities. She celebrated diversity and encouraged others to embrace their true selves without fear or shame.

Nyla's story serves as a reminder that coming out is a personal journey, and each individual's experience is unique. No two journeys are the same, and it is important to approach each person with empathy, respect, and love.

Unconventional Exercise: Write a letter to someone who has recently come out to you, offering your support, understanding, and love. Share any personal experiences or insights that may help them navigate their journey with confidence and resilience. As you write the letter, reflect on the importance of acceptance and the potential impact it can have on someone's life.

Remember, coming out is a continuous process, and it may take time for individuals to fully embrace and share their identities. Offer your unwavering support and remind them that they are not alone in their journey.

Nyla's reflections on mental health and self-care

Nyla Ashen, despite her remarkable achievements as an LGBTQ activist, understands the importance of taking care of her mental health and prioritizing self-care. In this section, we delve into Nyla's reflections on mental health and the strategies she employs to maintain a healthy balance between her activism and personal well-being.

Mental health is a topic close to Nyla's heart, as she has personally experienced the toll that discrimination and societal pressures can take on one's mental well-being. Nyla believes that it is crucial to address and destigmatize mental health issues within the LGBTQ community, as they often face additional challenges and stressors.

Nyla's reflections on mental health highlight the importance of seeking support and therapy. She emphasizes that therapy is not a sign of weakness, but rather a powerful tool for personal growth and self-discovery. Nyla openly discusses her own experiences with therapy, highlighting how it has helped her navigate the complexities of her identity and cope with the emotional burden of activism.

Moreover, Nyla believes that self-care is essential for maintaining mental and emotional well-being. She encourages individuals to prioritize self-care activities that bring them joy and peace, whether it's practicing yoga, engaging in creative outlets, or simply taking time to relax and rejuvenate. Nyla firmly believes that self-care is not selfish but rather a means of replenishing oneself and enabling one to be more effective in their activism.

In her reflections, Nyla also acknowledges the challenges of balancing activism with personal boundaries. She reminds readers that setting boundaries and taking breaks is crucial for maintaining mental health. Nyla often emphasizes the power of saying "no" and recognizing one's limits, even in the face of immense pressure. She reminds activists and individuals alike that taking care of their own well-being is not only necessary but also an act of resistance against societal norms that may disregard their mental health needs.

To illustrate the importance of mental health and self-care, Nyla shares anecdotes and real-life experiences of individuals who have faced burnout or struggled with their mental well-being within the LGBTQ community. These stories serve as a reminder of the ongoing battle for mental health support and the necessity of prioritizing self-care within the community.

Nyla also provides resources and practical tips for individuals seeking to improve their mental health and practice self-care. She emphasizes the benefits of mindfulness and meditation as tools for managing stress and anxiety. Additionally, she highlights the importance of finding supportive communities and spaces where individuals can freely express themselves and seek guidance.

In an unconventional yet captivating approach, Nyla includes a series of interactive exercises throughout this section. These exercises allow readers to engage with the text on a personal level, encouraging self-reflection and introspection. By incorporating these exercises, Nyla empowers individuals to take an active role in their mental well-being and practice self-care strategies that work for them.

As the chapter comes to a close, Nyla leaves readers with her most cherished advice – that taking care of one's mental health is a lifelong journey. She reminds us that it is okay to stumble and experience setbacks along the way, as long as we always prioritize our well-being and take the necessary steps towards self-care.

In conclusion, Nyla Ashen's reflections on mental health and self-care offer a valuable perspective on the challenges faced by LGBTQ activists. By openly addressing her own experiences and providing practical advice, Nyla demonstrates her commitment to destigmatizing mental health within the community. Her insights inspire individuals to prioritize self-care and seek support when needed, emphasizing that mental well-being is an essential aspect of effective activism and personal resilience.

Finding balance between activism and personal life

In order to be an effective LGBTQ activist, Nyla Ashen had to find a balance between her activism and her personal life. This section explores the challenges she faced and the strategies she developed to maintain this delicate balance.

The demand for constant activism

As an influential LGBTQ activist, Nyla Ashen was constantly in demand. She received requests for interviews, speaking engagements, and collaborations from various organizations. Her inbox was flooded with messages from LGBTQ youth seeking advice and support. While Nyla was grateful for the opportunities to make a difference, she quickly realized that she couldn't say yes to everything.

Setting boundaries and priorities

Nyla had to learn the art of setting boundaries and priorities. She recognized that her well-being and personal relationships were just as important as her activism. Nyla made a conscious decision to allocate time for self-care, family, and close friends to maintain a sense of balance in her life.

Time management and delegation

To handle the overwhelming demands on her time, Nyla became a master of time management. She carefully planned her schedule, setting aside designated hours for activism and ensuring that she had time for herself and her loved ones. Nyla also learned the importance of delegation, entrusting certain tasks to her team and fellow activists.

Self-care and mental health

Nyla understood that fighting for LGBTQ rights required not only physical energy but also emotional resilience. She made a point of prioritizing self-care and mental health. Nyla engaged in activities that brought her joy and allowed her to recharge, such as practicing yoga, meditating, and spending time in nature. She also sought therapy to process her emotions and handle the stresses of her activism.

Maintaining relationships

As an activist, Nyla often traveled extensively and was frequently away from her loved ones. This posed a challenge for maintaining healthy relationships. However,

SECTION THREE 89

Nyla was committed to nurturing her relationships and keeping her connections strong. She utilized technology to stay connected with her friends and family, regularly scheduling video calls or sending heartfelt messages.

Finding inspiration outside of activism

To prevent burnout, Nyla actively sought inspiration outside of her activism. She recognized the importance of pursuing hobbies and interests that were unrelated to her advocacy work. Whether it was painting, cooking, or immersing herself in literature, these activities provided her with a much-needed break and fresh perspective.

Creating a support network

Nyla understood the significance of surrounding herself with a strong support network. She cultivated relationships with other LGBTQ activists who could relate to her experiences and offer support. The camaraderie and shared purpose provided Nyla with the encouragement, advice, and understanding that she needed to continue her fight for LGBTQ rights.

The struggle for work-life balance

Finding a balance between activism and personal life was an ongoing challenge for Nyla. There were times when her workload became overwhelming, and she had to make sacrifices. However, Nyla continually reminded herself that she was not alone in this struggle and that it was essential to take care of herself in order to effectively advocate for others.

Unconventional trick: the power of saying no

One unconventional trick that Nyla learned along the way was the power of saying no. She realized that she couldn't be everywhere and do everything, and that saying no to certain opportunities or requests was not a sign of weakness. By selectively choosing where to direct her energy, Nyla was able to protect her own well-being and ensure that she could continue making a real impact in the areas that mattered most to her.

In conclusion, finding a balance between activism and personal life was a constant struggle for Nyla Ashen. Through setting boundaries, practicing self-care, surrounding herself with support, and learning the power of saying no, Nyla managed to navigate the demanding world of activism while maintaining her own well-being. Her journey serves as an example for future LGBTQ activists, reminding them of the importance of finding equilibrium in their pursuit of social change.

Conclusion

The Legacy of Nyla Ashen

Nyla's lasting impact on LGBTQ rights in Qirona

Nyla Ashen's fearless advocacy for LGBTQ rights in Qirona has left an indelible mark on the country's social and legal landscape. Through her tireless efforts, she has championed equality, challenged discrimination, and paved the way for a more inclusive society. Let us delve into Nyla's lasting impact on LGBTQ rights in Qirona and the transformative changes she has brought about.

One of Nyla's greatest achievements is her instrumental role in pushing for legislative change. She tirelessly fought for the repeal of discriminatory laws and policies that targeted the LGBTQ community. Nyla took to the streets, organized protests, and lobbied lawmakers to create a safer and more equitable society for all Qironans. Her influential voice and unyielding determination compelled the government to reassess its stance on LGBTQ rights.

The impact of Nyla's advocacy can be seen in the significant legal victories she achieved. Through her groundbreaking court cases, she successfully challenged the constitutionality of discriminatory laws, leading to their eventual repeal. Nyla's efforts have enshrined equal rights for LGBTQ individuals in Qirona's legal system, a monumental step toward complete inclusivity.

But Nyla's impact extends far beyond the courtroom. She recognized the importance of education in fostering acceptance and understanding of LGBTQ identities. To this end, she spearheaded initiatives promoting LGBTQ-inclusive education in schools and universities across Qirona. By working closely with educators and policymakers, she ensured that LGBTQ students and their experiences were respected and acknowledged within the educational system.

Nyla's influence transcended national boundaries and reached the global stage. Her international recognition as a leading LGBTQ activist provided a platform for her to advocate for change worldwide. She delivered powerful keynote speeches at LGBTQ conferences, sharing her experiences and strategies to empower activists in other countries. Nyla's efforts have inspired a new generation of activists, igniting a global movement for LGBTQ rights.

Moreover, Nyla's impact on public opinion cannot be overstated. She played a crucial role in shifting societal attitudes toward greater acceptance and equality. Through interviews on television shows and social media platforms, Nyla debunked myths and misconceptions, humanizing the experiences of LGBTQ individuals. Her open and honest discussions challenged deeply ingrained biases, fostering empathy and understanding among Qirona's general population.

Nyla's lasting impact on LGBTQ rights in Qirona can also be measured by the changes she has brought about within the entertainment industry. By forming alliances with LGBTQ celebrities, she ensured representation and visibility of LGBTQ individuals on screens both big and small. Nyla's collaborations with influential LGBTQ influencers helped dismantle stereotypes and fostered a more inclusive media landscape, encouraging young LGBTQ individuals to embrace their own identities.

But Nyla's journey has not been without its challenges. The path she carved was often met with resistance, criticism, and controversy. Yet, she remained resilient, using her wit and humor to disarm her detractors. Nyla's ability to navigate these obstacles with grace and determination has inspired countless LGBTQ individuals to stand up for their rights, even in the face of adversity.

As we celebrate Nyla's trailblazing journey, we must remember that the fight for LGBTQ rights is far from over. Nyla herself acknowledges that her work is just a stepping stone toward a future where every individual can live free from discrimination and prejudice. Her lasting impact on LGBTQ rights in Qirona serves as a reminder that change is possible, and it is up to each of us to continue her legacy by actively advocating for a more inclusive and equitable society.

In conclusion, Nyla Ashen's unwavering dedication to LGBTQ rights in Qirona has had a profound and lasting impact. Through her activism, she has not only challenged discriminatory laws and policies but also reshaped societal attitudes and fostered acceptance. Nyla's influence extends beyond Qirona's borders, inspiring activists worldwide and igniting a global movement for LGBTQ rights. Her legacy serves as a reminder that with passion, resilience, and unwavering determination, lasting change is achievable.

The continued fight for equality and acceptance

The fight for equality and acceptance in the LGBTQ community is an ongoing battle that requires continuous effort and dedication. Despite the significant progress that has been made in recent years, there are still many challenges that need to be addressed. In this section, we will explore some of the key issues that the LGBTQ community faces today and discuss the strategies and initiatives that can help further the cause of equality and acceptance.

Challenging discrimination and prejudice

Discrimination and prejudice remain major obstacles in the path towards full LGBTQ acceptance. Many individuals still face discrimination based on their sexual orientation or gender identity in various aspects of their lives, including employment, housing, and healthcare. It is crucial to continue advocating for legislation and policies that prohibit discrimination based on sexual orientation and gender identity, both at the local and national levels.

One effective strategy is to raise awareness about the experiences of LGBTQ individuals and humanize their stories. Sharing personal narratives and highlighting the contributions of LGBTQ individuals in various fields can help challenge stereotypes and promote a more inclusive society. Educational initiatives targeted at schools and workplaces can also play a significant role in fostering understanding, empathy, and respect for diversity.

Addressing intersectional issues

It is important to recognize that LGBTQ individuals can face multiple forms of discrimination due to the intersection of their sexual orientation or gender identity with other aspects of their identity, such as race, ethnicity, socio-economic status, or disability. Intersectionality acknowledges the complex and interconnected nature of different forms of oppression and discrimination.

To effectively address intersectional issues, it is crucial for LGBTQ activists to ally themselves with other social justice movements and work towards collective liberation. By collaborating with organizations that fight against racism, sexism, and ableism, the LGBTQ community can amplify its message and make significant progress in dismantling systems of oppression.

Promoting LGBTQ-inclusive education

Education is an essential tool for creating a more inclusive society. LGBTQ-inclusive education plays a vital role in challenging heteronormativity and cisnormativity, and promoting acceptance and understanding among young people. By integrating LGBTQ history, literature, and experiences into the curriculum, schools can help eliminate stereotypes and foster an environment where LGBTQ students feel seen, valued, and supported.

Providing resources and training for educators is crucial to ensure that they have the knowledge and skills to address the specific needs and challenges faced by LGBTQ students. Additionally, implementing anti-bullying policies and support systems within schools can create a safe and inclusive environment for all students.

Supporting mental health and well-being

The LGBTQ community continues to face higher rates of mental health challenges compared to the general population. The stigmatization and discrimination experienced by LGBTQ individuals can have a significant impact on their mental well-being. It is essential to prioritize mental health support and resources that are specifically tailored to the needs of the LGBTQ community.

Creating safe spaces and support networks where LGBTQ individuals can connect with others who share similar experiences can be beneficial in promoting their mental health and well-being. LGBTQ-inclusive therapy and counseling services can also provide vital support for individuals navigating the challenges of coming out, facing discrimination, or dealing with internalized homophobia or transphobia.

Global advocacy for LGBTQ rights

While progress has been made towards LGBTQ acceptance in many parts of the world, there are still numerous countries where same-sex relationships are criminalized and LGBTQ individuals face severe persecution. Global advocacy is crucial to supporting and amplifying the voices of LGBTQ activists in these regions and holding governments accountable for human rights violations.

Supporting grassroots organizations, providing financial assistance, and raising awareness about LGBTQ issues on an international level can help bring about significant change. International pressure and diplomatic efforts can be powerful tools in urging governments to decriminalize homosexuality, protect LGBTQ individuals from violence and discrimination, and promote equality and acceptance.

In conclusion, the fight for equality and acceptance in the LGBTQ community is an ongoing struggle that requires persistent activism and advocacy. By challenging discrimination, addressing intersectional issues, promoting LGBTQ-inclusive education, supporting mental health and well-being, and engaging in global advocacy, we can continue to make progress towards a more inclusive and accepting world for all LGBTQ individuals. Together, we can create a future where everyone can live authentically and with dignity, regardless of their sexual orientation or gender identity.

Nyla's Words of Inspiration for the Next Generation

As Nyla Ashen reflects on her incredible journey as an LGBTQ activist in Qirona, she finds herself overwhelmed with gratitude and hope for the future. In this final section, Nyla shares her words of inspiration and wisdom for the next generation, who will continue the fight for equality and acceptance.

Embrace Your Authenticity

Nyla believes that the first step towards creating a more inclusive society is for individuals to fully embrace their authentic selves. She encourages the next generation to explore their identities and find the courage to express who they truly are. Nyla emphasizes that it is not only important to accept oneself, but to also celebrate the unique qualities that make each individual special.

"Embrace your authenticity. Your true self is your greatest strength. When you embrace who you are and live your truth, you inspire others to do the same. Never be afraid to shine brightly and show the world your beautiful colors." ([?])

Educate and Empower

Education plays a crucial role in creating a more inclusive and accepting society. Nyla encourages the next generation to educate themselves about LGBTQ history, rights, and issues. She believes that knowledge is power and that by equipping themselves with the facts, they can effectively challenge stereotypes and prejudices.

Furthermore, Nyla emphasizes that education should not be limited to oneself, but should also be used to empower others. She urges the next generation to become advocates for LGBTQ rights by sharing their knowledge and experiences, fostering understanding, and standing up against discrimination.

> Education is our greatest weapon against ignorance and discrimination. Arm yourselves with knowledge, and wield it to

dismantle the barriers that prevent us from achieving true equality. By educating ourselves and others, we can create a world where every individual is respected, valued, and celebrated for who they are. ([?])

Build Bridges and Foster Alliances

In her journey as an activist, Nyla has witnessed the power of building bridges and fostering alliances with others. She believes that true progress can only be achieved through collaboration, understanding, and unity.

Nyla encourages the next generation to reach out to different communities, organizations, and individuals who may not necessarily share their backgrounds or perspectives. She stresses that by finding common ground and working together, they can create a more inclusive society that celebrates the diverse tapestry of humanity.

> Building bridges between communities is essential in dismantling social barriers and fostering a more inclusive society. By embracing our differences, engaging in meaningful dialogue, and finding common goals, we can create a world where love and acceptance trump hate and discrimination. Together, we are stronger. ([?])

Persist in the Face of Adversity

Throughout her activism, Nyla has faced numerous challenges, setbacks, and moments of doubt. However, she believes that the key to making a lasting impact is to persist despite the adversity.

Nyla wants the next generation to understand that the path to change is often difficult, but it is worth fighting for. She encourages them to stay true to their mission, even when faced with opposition, and to have unwavering faith in their ability to effect change.

> Remember, change does not happen overnight. It requires resilience, determination, and unwavering faith in your cause. When faced with adversity, find strength in your convictions, and let it fuel your determination to create a better world. Every small step forward counts. ([?])

Spread Love and Kindness

In a world filled with division and hate, Nyla believes that love and kindness are revolutionary acts. She encourages the next generation to approach their activism with compassion and empathy, and to be catalysts for positive change.

Nyla reminds them that true progress is not only measured in policy changes but also in the hearts and minds of individuals. She encourages a culture of respect, understanding, and love, as these qualities have the power to transform lives and create lasting change.

> Spread love and kindness wherever you go. Your actions, no matter how small, have the power to create a ripple effect that transcends boundaries and transforms lives. Be a beacon of light in a world that sometimes feels dark, and let your love be the force that changes hearts and minds. ([?])

Conclusion

As Nyla Ashen concludes her inspiring biography, she leaves the readers with a sense of hope and determination. Through her journey, she has shown that one person's unwavering commitment to change can make a significant impact on society. Nyla's words of inspiration, rooted in her own experiences, resonate deeply with the next generation of LGBTQ activists, who will continue to fight for equality, acceptance, and love. Together, they will carry the torch, ensuring that progress is not only sustained but also expanded upon. As we celebrate Nyla's trailblazing journey, we are reminded that, with passion and determination, we can all contribute to a brighter and more inclusive future.

A glimpse into Nyla's future endeavors

As Nyla Ashen continues to make waves and break barriers in the LGBTQ community, her future endeavors hold great promise. With her tireless dedication and unwavering passion for equality and acceptance, Nyla is poised to make an even greater impact in the years to come. Here, we take a look at what the future may hold for this trailblazing activist.

One of Nyla's primary goals for the future is to expand her advocacy on a global scale. She plans to broaden her reach and collaborate with LGBTQ activists from around the world. By forging alliances and sharing knowledge, Nyla aims to create a unified front in the fight for LGBTQ rights and liberation.

To further amplify her message, Nyla aspires to explore different mediums of storytelling. She envisions using her writing skills to pen a memoir, sharing her personal journey, triumphs, and challenges as an LGBTQ activist. Through her words, she hopes to inspire others to embrace their identities and stand up for what they believe in.

In addition to her writing endeavors, Nyla intends to delve into the world of filmmaking. She sees the power of visual storytelling as a means to educate, engage, and inspire change. Nyla envisions producing a documentary that highlights the intersectionality of LGBTQ identities, shedding light on the diverse experiences within the community.

Nyla recognizes the importance of education in driving social change. Moving forward, she plans to establish a foundation dedicated to providing scholarships for LGBTQ youth pursuing higher education. By removing financial barriers, Nyla hopes to empower the next generation of activists and leaders, ensuring that their voices are heard and their dreams realized.

In her quest for equality, Nyla aims to influence policy and legislation on a national level. She plans to run for political office, using her platform to enact change from within the system. Nyla's comprehensive understanding of LGBTQ issues, combined with her charisma and tenacity, make her a formidable force in shaping laws that protect and uplift marginalized communities.

As she sets her sights on the future, Nyla remains committed to nurturing her mental health and well-being. She recognizes the importance of self-care and intends to prioritize it in her daily life. By practicing mindfulness, engaging in creative outlets, and surrounding herself with a supportive network, Nyla strives to maintain a healthy balance between her activism and personal life.

While uncertainties and challenges lie ahead, Nyla Ashen approaches the future with hope, determination, and resilience. By continuing to be a beacon of empowerment and a force for positive change, Nyla is poised to leave an indelible mark on the world. As she paves the way for a more inclusive future, her influence will undoubtedly shape the lives of LGBTQ individuals for generations to come.

Stay tuned for the next chapter in Nyla Ashen's remarkable journey – a journey that holds the promise of a brighter, more inclusive future.

THE LEGACY OF NYLA ASHEN

Celebrating Nyla's trailblazing journey

In this final section, we celebrate the incredible journey of Nyla Ashen and the lasting impact she has made on LGBTQ rights in Qirona and beyond. Her trailblazing efforts have not only broken barriers but also inspired a new generation of activists and advocates for equality and acceptance.

Nyla's journey has been one of resilience, courage, and unwavering determination. Throughout her career as an LGBTQ activist, she has overcome countless obstacles and faced opposition with humor, wit, and grace. Her unique approach to advocacy has set her apart and made her a force to be reckoned with in the LGBTQ community.

One of the many aspects that make Nyla's journey so remarkable is her groundbreaking LGBTQ campaign. Through her campaign, she has raised awareness and challenged societal norms, pushing the boundaries of acceptance and understanding. Despite facing opposition and backlash, Nyla's campaign milestones stand as a testament to her unwavering spirit and commitment to progress.

Nyla's impact extends beyond traditional media platforms. She has utilized social media as a powerful tool to amplify her message and reach a global audience. Her viral social media moments have sparked important conversations and shed light on the importance of representation in the media. Nyla's collaborations with LGBTQ influencers have further expanded her reach and united voices in the fight for equality.

In addition to her media presence, Nyla has formed alliances with LGBTQ celebrities, recognizing the significance of LGBTQ representation in the entertainment industry. Through these alliances, she has not only increased visibility but also dismantled stereotypes and challenged heteronormativity. Despite rumors and controversies surrounding her relationships, Nyla's focus has always remained on her advocacy work and the betterment of LGBTQ youth around the world.

Perhaps one of the most remarkable aspects of Nyla's journey is her fight for LGBTQ rights in Qirona. Challenging discriminatory laws and policies, she has been at the forefront of legal battles and efforts to promote LGBTQ-inclusive education. The impact of Nyla's advocacy on the legal system is undeniable, and her groundbreaking court cases have set precedents for future generations.

Nyla's dedication and passion have garnered international recognition and accolades. She has received numerous awards and honors for her activism, and her keynote speeches at LGBTQ conferences worldwide have inspired countless individuals to stand up for their rights. Nyla's global impact is immeasurable, as she has become a symbol of hope and resilience for LGBTQ communities around the world.

Beyond her achievements as an activist, Nyla's personal struggles and triumphs have shaped her journey. Navigating relationships and love as an LGBTQ activist comes with its own set of challenges, but Nyla's authenticity and openness have paved the way for others to embrace their true selves. Coming out to her family and community was not without its difficulties, but Nyla's courage has empowered others to do the same.

Throughout her journey, Nyla has emphasized the importance of mental health and self-care for activists. She has openly reflected on her own experiences, normalizing discussions around mental health and inspiring others to prioritize their well-being. Finding balance between activism and personal life is an ongoing process, and Nyla's insights serve as a guiding light for those who follow in her footsteps.

As we celebrate Nyla Ashen's trailblazing journey, it is essential to recognize that her legacy extends far beyond her individual achievements. Her impact on LGBTQ rights in Qirona will continue to reverberate for generations to come. The fight for equality and acceptance is ongoing, and Nyla's words of inspiration serve as a call to action for the next generation of activists.

In her future endeavors, Nyla Ashen will undoubtedly continue to break barriers, challenge norms, and advocate for a more inclusive and accepting world. Her trailblazing journey has paved the way for progress, and her legacy will forever inspire and empower those who continue the fight for LGBTQ rights.

Together, let us celebrate Nyla's unstoppable spirit, her unwavering dedication, and her profound impact on the LGBTQ community. Her journey is a testament to the power of one individual to effect change, and her legacy will forever shine as a beacon of hope and inspiration.

Index

-doubt, 3

ability, 4, 9, 11, 15, 28, 29, 31, 32, 34–36, 38, 42, 44, 48, 49, 65, 68–72, 74, 76–78, 81, 92, 96
ableism, 93
absurdity, 33
acceptance, 1–14, 16, 17, 19, 21, 23–26, 28, 30–33, 35, 36, 38–41, 43–50, 52, 56–61, 64–66, 69, 71, 72, 74, 75, 77–86, 91–95, 97, 99, 100
access, 18, 66, 67, 85
acclaim, 45
accolade, 68, 70
achievement, 30
act, 23, 55, 65, 83, 87
action, 8, 9, 31, 42, 43, 49, 65, 73, 77, 82, 100
activism, 3–6, 8–11, 14–19, 24, 25, 29, 31, 33–35, 37, 38, 41–44, 46–48, 55, 66, 68–83, 86–89, 92, 95–100
activist, 1, 2, 4, 5, 9–11, 14, 15, 23, 26, 28, 30, 33–36, 42, 46–48, 56, 57, 68, 78, 79, 81–86, 88, 91, 95–100
actor, 43
addition, 5, 12, 33, 37, 49, 59, 62, 69, 71, 73, 78, 98, 99
address, 11, 13, 17, 24, 28, 29, 33, 34, 42, 62, 63, 81, 85, 86, 93, 94
admiration, 5
adolescence, 2
adoption, 65
advantage, 34
adversity, 3, 4, 6–9, 33, 48, 50, 68, 72, 75, 77, 78, 80, 92, 96
advice, 7, 12, 30, 37, 85, 87–89
advocacy, 4, 5, 8–17, 19, 23, 26, 27, 29, 30, 35, 41–44, 47, 48, 51, 52, 56, 59, 61, 63–66, 68–71, 73–75, 77, 79, 85, 89, 91, 94, 95, 97, 99
advocate, 1, 4, 6, 18, 19, 26, 29, 30, 32, 38, 40, 43, 44, 58, 59, 61, 64, 65, 69, 71, 76, 84, 89, 92, 100
affection, 83
age, 1, 2, 7, 41, 59, 61, 63, 77
agenda, 33, 41
Alan Downs, 83
Alex, 4
Alex Diaz, 4

alliance, 10, 43, 44
ally, 44, 93
allyship, 22, 27, 77
amendment, 59
amplification, 19, 26, 27
anecdote, 50
anger, 8, 10, 13
anxiety, 87
appearance, 32, 34, 35
applause, 49
appreciation, 2, 63
approach, 5, 9, 10, 15–17, 19, 22, 24, 25, 28–30, 36, 37, 40, 42, 47–49, 51, 56, 58, 65, 71, 72, 74, 76, 77, 84, 86, 87, 97, 99
area, 79
art, 8, 16, 18, 24, 40, 57, 74, 88
article, 30
artist, 4, 25
artivism, 25
Ashen, 65
aspect, 21, 23, 65, 74, 83, 87
assistance, 69, 85, 94
attention, 10, 12, 15, 16, 19, 29–32, 42–44, 46, 48, 50, 55, 67, 71, 75
attitude, 4
audience, 7, 18, 19, 22, 23, 25, 28, 29, 32–37, 40, 43, 49–51, 59, 72–74, 76, 78, 81, 99
authenticity, 4, 5, 11, 16, 17, 19, 35, 36, 39, 41, 43, 47, 63, 80, 85, 100
award, 68, 70, 71
awareness, 12, 13, 15, 19, 21–23, 29–32, 34, 37, 40, 41, 43, 44, 48, 55, 57–59, 61, 63, 65, 66, 75, 85, 93, 94, 99

backdrop, 9
background, 19, 73
backlash, 10, 23–25, 27, 80, 83, 99
balance, 11, 14, 15, 30, 80–82, 86, 88, 89, 98, 100
ballroom, 45
ban, 67
banter, 35
battle, 57, 67, 78, 87, 93
beacon, 6, 35, 48, 52, 57, 76, 81, 98, 100
beauty, 37, 38
Becky Albertalli, 45
beginning, 2, 18
behavior, 63
being, 1, 8, 11, 12, 15, 24, 34, 38, 39, 47, 48, 65, 66, 69, 70, 76, 79–84, 86–90, 94, 95, 98, 100
belief, 4, 50
belonging, 4, 12, 14–16, 25, 26, 32, 40, 41, 45, 62, 76
benefit, 61
betterment, 99
bigotry, 6
binary, 3, 6, 30, 47
biography, 97
biphobia, 47
bisexuality, 47
blend, 2, 29, 36, 48, 71
board, 66
bond, 12
box, 16, 71
brainstorm, 29
bravery, 4, 11, 32, 68
break, 3, 6, 7, 13, 14, 18, 25, 26, 28, 39, 41, 51, 63, 71, 77, 80, 85, 86, 89, 97, 100
breeding, 63

Index 103

bridge, 10, 18, 25–28
bucket, 23
building, 5, 7, 25, 26, 59, 73, 77, 81, 96
bullying, 61, 63, 64, 75, 94
burden, 86
burnout, 80, 87, 89

call, 24, 100
camaraderie, 5, 89
campaign, 10, 14, 21–23, 27, 30, 31, 36, 42, 57, 61, 99
care, 8, 11, 15, 76, 80, 81, 86–89, 98, 100
career, 4, 5, 15, 99
case, 56, 65–67, 74
casting, 39
catalyst, 3, 6, 21, 37, 40, 51, 81
cause, 10–12, 14, 18, 26, 27, 29, 31, 41, 43, 44, 77, 81, 82, 93
celebration, 76
celebrity, 43
center, 46
challenge, 1, 3, 4, 8, 9, 13, 14, 18, 19, 21–27, 29, 30, 33, 39–41, 43–46, 50, 55, 58, 60, 63, 64, 66, 68, 70–72, 79–81, 83, 85, 88, 89, 93, 95, 100
change, 2, 4–12, 15, 17, 19, 21–23, 25–33, 35, 37, 40, 41, 43, 44, 48–51, 55, 57–59, 65, 68–74, 77, 80–82, 85, 90–92, 94, 96–98, 100
chapter, 14, 72
character, 45
charisma, 77, 98
charm, 76
child, 6
childhood, 1, 9

cisnormativity, 94
citizenship, 63
city, 2, 12, 25
clarity, 80
classroom, 62
cleverness, 28
client, 67
close, 1, 79, 86, 88
closing, 51
coalition, 22, 25, 26
collaboration, 17, 18, 22, 23, 25, 31, 39–44, 64, 73–75, 96
color, 76
combat, 24, 25, 38, 71
combination, 23
comeback, 28, 29
comedy, 17, 19, 27
comfort, 79, 83
commentary, 8
commitment, 4, 10, 15, 16, 18, 19, 27, 31, 33, 41, 44, 47, 48, 52, 67, 68, 70, 77, 78, 83, 87, 97, 99
communication, 48, 73, 82
community, 1–7, 10–14, 16–19, 21, 23, 25–41, 43–50, 55, 57, 59, 61, 63–66, 68–74, 76–80, 82, 84–87, 91, 93–95, 97–100
compassion, 1, 7, 8, 24, 50, 70, 72, 97
complexity, 79, 82
compromise, 83
concern, 33
concert, 44
conclusion, 5, 15, 17, 19, 40, 48, 52, 66, 76, 87, 89, 92, 95
conflict, 24
confrontation, 10, 13

confusion, 6, 79
connection, 28, 35, 50, 72
constitutionality, 67, 91
content, 17, 23, 37, 42, 45, 46
context, 48
controversy, 92
conversation, 10, 16, 33–35, 84
cooking, 89
counseling, 22, 85, 94
country, 4, 23, 57, 59, 74, 91
courage, 2–4, 15, 35, 67, 68, 75, 79, 82, 84, 95, 99, 100
course, 29
court, 15, 56, 65–67, 74, 91, 99
courtroom, 66, 67, 91
coverage, 33
creation, 27, 37
creative, 17, 23, 33, 39, 46, 71, 72, 74, 87, 98
creativity, 2, 4, 8, 13, 16, 22, 24
credibility, 18, 49
criticism, 28, 29, 92
culmination, 56
culture, 8, 18, 45, 66, 97
curiosity, 1, 2, 9, 50
curricula, 13, 19, 30, 56, 62, 71, 75
curriculum, 59, 61, 64–66, 94
cycle, 55

dance, 40, 74
data, 48–51, 73, 74
day, 23
daytime, 31
debate, 33, 47
decision, 11, 31, 56, 58, 67, 73, 88
dedication, 4, 14, 15, 17, 27, 31, 43, 64, 68–72, 75–78, 80, 82, 83, 92, 93, 97, 99, 100
delegation, 88

demand, 16, 43, 46, 65, 88
demeanor, 34
demonstration, 83
designer, 44
desire, 1, 2, 9, 11, 50
determination, 3–7, 9, 15, 17, 19, 23, 25, 31, 35, 56, 57, 69, 71, 72, 77, 85, 91, 92, 97–99
development, 4, 45, 65
dialogue, 7, 16, 22–24, 27–29, 31, 34–36, 39, 43, 57, 64, 65, 70, 77, 84, 85
difference, 6, 9, 14, 35, 70, 74, 78, 88
dignity, 1, 24, 28, 57, 72, 95
direction, 25
disability, 42, 93
disapproval, 6
discourse, 59
discovery, 2, 3, 6, 8, 9, 12, 15, 16, 34, 43, 47, 72, 77, 86
discrimination, 1, 5–9, 21, 22, 24–26, 30, 31, 34, 44, 49–51, 55, 56, 58, 59, 61–67, 71–73, 75–81, 84–86, 91–95
discussion, 32, 84
dismantling, 10, 31, 40, 57, 73, 93
diversity, 1, 8, 11, 16, 18, 21, 23, 26, 32, 37, 38, 51, 64, 76, 86, 93
division, 97
documentary, 98
documentation, 56
domain, 56
doubt, 3, 96
down, 2, 6, 8, 13–16, 18, 19, 25–32, 35, 39–42, 45, 48, 51, 63, 65, 67, 75, 77, 81, 85, 86

drama, 47
drive, 6, 9, 12, 26, 29, 36, 44, 59
dynamic, 49

ear, 12
ease, 28
education, 12, 13, 17, 19, 27, 30, 33–35, 37, 39, 55, 57, 59–66, 69, 71, 75–77, 84, 91, 94, 95, 98, 99
effect, 9, 15, 30–33, 35, 65, 70, 77, 96, 100
effort, 93
element, 17
eloquence, 11, 31, 34, 35
Elysia, 74
embrace, 2–4, 8, 11, 14, 16, 32, 39, 41, 43, 48–52, 56, 72, 75, 77, 78, 80–82, 84–86, 92, 95, 98, 100
empathy, 1, 5, 7–9, 13, 16, 18, 19, 21–23, 25, 27–30, 32, 34, 36–40, 44, 48, 49, 56–58, 61, 63–66, 72, 75, 82, 85, 86, 92, 93, 97
emphasis, 21, 76
employment, 31, 56, 58, 66, 93
empowerment, 26, 51, 52, 81, 85, 98
encounter, 3
encourage, 27, 49, 58, 73
encouragement, 7, 78, 89
end, 29, 91
endeavor, 37
energy, 25, 80, 88, 89
engagement, 12, 19, 37, 51, 57, 65
entertainment, 10, 27, 37, 44–46, 92, 99
enthusiasm, 21

environment, 1, 2, 22, 27, 56, 61, 66, 94
equality, 2, 4–12, 14–17, 19, 21, 23, 25, 26, 28, 30–33, 38, 40–44, 46, 48, 52, 56–60, 64, 66–72, 74, 78, 79, 82, 83, 91–95, 97–100
equilibrium, 80, 90
escape, 37
essay, 23
essence, 32, 40
esteem, 15, 38
ethnicity, 73, 93
event, 83
evidence, 22, 24, 49, 73
example, 23, 33, 34, 39, 40, 42, 45, 64, 74, 77, 81, 90
exception, 80
exclusion, 9, 61
exercise, 8
exhibit, 68
existence, 1
experience, 14, 16, 35, 49, 63, 74, 84–86
expert, 66
expertise, 44
exploration, 39
expression, 2, 6, 24, 46, 74
eye, 47, 82

face, 4, 7, 8, 23, 48, 50, 68, 72, 75–78, 80, 81, 86, 87, 92–94
fact, 32, 82
faculty, 19
faith, 22, 24, 96
fame, 10, 15, 44
family, 2, 7, 10, 11, 14, 24, 49, 79, 82, 84, 85, 88, 89, 100

fashion, 18, 44
favor, 65–67
fear, 2, 26, 39, 50, 72, 79, 83, 84, 86
feeling, 83
feminism, 3
fight, 1, 4–6, 8, 11, 13, 14, 16, 17, 23, 26, 27, 33, 41, 43, 48, 53, 55, 57, 59, 60, 64, 66–70, 72, 74, 76–78, 80–82, 89, 92, 93, 95, 97, 99, 100
fighting, 2, 6, 10, 11, 15, 28, 29, 46, 56, 68, 76, 80, 88, 96
figure, 4, 15, 17, 23, 38, 43, 46, 47
film, 43, 45
filmmaking, 98
finding, 3, 5, 7, 10, 18, 50, 79, 81–83, 87, 89, 90, 96
fire, 6
flame, 1
flash, 16
fluidity, 3
focus, 47, 48, 80, 99
force, 7, 29, 57, 98, 99
forefront, 2, 9, 15, 68, 99
form, 25, 35
format, 23
foster, 8–11, 13, 19, 21, 28, 29, 40, 41, 43, 45, 46, 61, 63, 65, 70, 73, 77, 94
foundation, 2, 5, 6, 64, 80, 83, 98
framework, 58
freedom, 2, 67
frenzy, 47
front, 25, 41, 43, 97
fuel, 6, 8, 77
fulfillment, 15
fund, 69

future, 2, 5, 6, 9, 11, 14, 17, 23, 25, 28, 31, 33, 35, 39, 44, 50, 51, 53, 57, 60, 64–66, 69, 72, 75, 76, 78, 90, 92, 95, 97–100

game, 37
gap, 18, 22, 25, 26
gender, 1–3, 6, 7, 9, 13, 16, 24, 28, 30, 40–42, 45, 51, 55, 56, 59–62, 66, 67, 79, 93, 95
generation, 17, 35, 55, 59, 64, 67, 82, 92, 95–100
globe, 4, 36
goal, 13
gossip, 46, 47
government, 31, 58, 59, 91
grace, 18, 28, 92, 99
grade, 61, 64
grandmother, 1
gratitude, 35, 95
gravity, 29, 49
ground, 2, 27, 28, 35, 50, 96
groundbreaking, 10, 14, 15, 21, 23, 30, 41, 56, 65–69, 71, 74, 91, 99
group, 12, 13, 73
growth, 8, 15, 17, 33, 47, 48, 50, 81–83, 86
guidance, 5, 7, 12, 17, 62, 76, 85, 87

hand, 49
happiness, 47, 67
harassment, 24, 63
hardship, 7
harm, 7, 39
Harper, 43
Harper Thompson, 43
Harvey Milk, 68

hashtag, 36
hate, 6, 24, 97
hatred, 50, 80
haven, 3
head, 50, 55
health, 11, 24, 66, 76, 79, 80, 82, 85–88, 94, 95, 98, 100
healthcare, 22, 93
hearing, 63
heart, 79, 86
heartwarming, 45, 50
help, 38, 57, 58, 83, 93, 94
heteronormativity, 94, 99
high, 44
hindrance, 6
history, 7, 13, 19, 61, 65, 66, 75, 94, 95
hit, 36, 45
home, 36, 57
hometown, 11
homophobia, 38, 62, 94
homosexuality, 24, 74, 94
honesty, 81
honor, 70
hope, 3, 6, 8, 9, 11, 17, 25, 35, 37, 41, 44, 48, 50–52, 55, 75–78, 80, 81, 95, 97, 98, 100
host, 33, 44
hostility, 33, 85
housing, 31, 58, 93
humanity, 28, 37, 57, 96
humility, 18
humor, 8, 10, 13, 17, 19, 25, 27–30, 33, 35–37, 71, 92, 99
hype, 47

ice, 23
icon, 43

idea, 23
identity, 2–9, 11, 13, 14, 24, 28, 30, 40, 45, 50, 51, 56, 59, 60, 62, 66, 67, 77, 79, 81, 83, 84, 86, 93, 95
ignorance, 7, 85
image, 35
impact, 2, 4, 6, 8–10, 12, 13, 15, 17, 18, 21, 23, 24, 30, 31, 33, 34, 36, 38, 39, 41–44, 46, 48–51, 56, 58, 62, 64, 66, 68–82, 84, 89, 91, 92, 94, 96, 97, 99, 100
implementation, 23, 30, 67
importance, 3–8, 10, 11, 13, 17, 18, 21, 23, 24, 26, 30, 32, 34, 36, 40, 41, 45, 47–51, 57–59, 61, 62, 65–67, 72, 73, 76, 77, 79–91, 98–100
impression, 51, 74
improvement, 27
inbox, 88
inception, 21
inclusion, 30
inclusivity, 3, 10, 12, 16, 19, 22, 24, 26, 32, 33, 39, 41–46, 61, 64, 68, 73, 76, 83, 91
incorporation, 74
individual, 4, 9, 24, 35, 37, 47, 49, 50, 57, 72, 78, 84, 86, 92, 95, 100
individuality, 2
industry, 10, 27, 44–46, 92, 99
inequality, 49, 73
influence, 3, 5, 7, 11, 14, 26, 31, 34, 35, 41, 44, 52, 68, 75, 77, 79, 91, 92, 98
influencer, 42
information, 47, 61, 66, 84

initiative, 18, 57
injustice, 6, 55
innovation, 8
insight, 5
inspiration, 2–6, 9, 15, 28, 31, 41, 48, 50, 51, 57, 66, 77, 82, 83, 85, 89, 95, 97, 100
instance, 45, 56, 65
instant, 36
intent, 30
interconnectedness, 3
intersection, 93
intersectionality, 3, 4, 36, 73, 98
interview, 31, 33, 35
intimacy, 37
intolerance, 5
introspection, 3, 27, 87
invisibility, 38
involvement, 12, 13, 26, 69, 74
irony, 25
issue, 24, 29, 46, 49, 58, 63

Jenna Martinez, 44
job, 56, 66
journalism, 47
journey, 2–17, 19, 24, 26, 28, 30, 31, 33–36, 43, 44, 46, 47, 49, 50, 56, 60, 67, 68, 72, 76–86, 90, 92, 95–100
joy, 79, 80, 82, 83, 87, 88
judgment, 3, 48, 83
Juno Dawson, 83
justice, 9, 25, 42, 55, 56, 64, 65, 67, 72, 93

key, 7, 15, 18, 21, 23, 25, 26, 31, 38, 44, 46, 51, 58, 64, 80, 81, 83, 93, 96
keynote, 72–74, 76, 92, 99

kindness, 97
knack, 21
knowledge, 7, 17, 27, 62, 94, 95, 97

landmark, 56, 65, 67
landscape, 5, 21, 23, 25, 33, 58, 59, 64, 91, 92
language, 25
laughter, 13, 28, 35
law, 4, 15, 55, 58, 66, 67, 74
layer, 79, 82
leader, 69, 77
leadership, 27, 68–71, 77
learning, 14, 61, 64, 66, 89
legacy, 5, 9, 64, 66, 67, 69, 76, 78, 82, 92, 100
legislation, 22, 24, 30, 55, 58, 74, 93, 98
lesson, 63
level, 21, 25, 38, 39, 72, 77, 81, 87, 94, 98
levity, 29, 71
liberation, 93, 97
life, 4, 5, 7, 10, 11, 14–16, 22, 33, 34, 36, 44, 46, 47, 58, 63, 75, 79–82, 84, 87–89, 98, 100
light, 9, 19, 28, 35, 37, 43, 48, 59, 74–76, 82, 98–100
limelight, 15
line, 29, 50
listening, 12
literature, 89, 94
litigation, 58, 64, 65
live, 4, 9, 60, 77, 80, 92, 95
look, 49, 97
loss, 56
love, 6, 8, 11, 24, 25, 44–51, 57, 60, 78–80, 82–86, 97, 100

Index

mainstream, 18, 32, 35, 38, 45, 51, 75
makeover, 45
making, 10, 15, 19, 26, 28, 31, 34, 35, 38, 44, 73, 78, 89, 96
man, 58
management, 88
manner, 8, 27
marathon, 80
marginalization, 38, 66
mark, 14, 31, 35, 59, 66, 72, 74, 76, 78, 82, 91, 98
marriage, 56, 58, 59, 67
master, 88
matter, 38, 77
means, 4, 29, 30, 59, 71, 87, 98
medal, 68
media, 10, 11, 15, 17, 22, 23, 30–33, 36, 38–48, 51, 59, 63, 65, 68, 71, 75, 76, 78, 80, 92, 99
meditating, 88
meditation, 87
medium, 40
member, 84
memoir, 98
mentor, 12
mentoring, 52
mentorship, 5, 17, 22, 62
message, 10, 12, 13, 18, 22, 28, 30, 33–36, 38, 43, 44, 48, 49, 59, 61, 72, 93, 98, 99
Mia, 42, 43
Mia Lopez, 42
microscope, 46
midst, 7, 76
milestone, 31
mindfulness, 8, 87, 98
mindset, 2, 13

misrepresentation, 33, 39
mission, 3, 12, 55, 85, 96
misunderstanding, 84
mobilization, 73
model, 4, 38, 48, 68, 77
moment, 11
momentum, 36
movement, 2, 9, 15, 17, 23, 24, 27, 68, 69, 73, 92
movie, 45
multimedia, 49
music, 18, 24, 40, 43, 45, 74
musician, 43

name, 18, 19
narrative, 16, 19, 25, 46, 47, 72, 81
nation, 67
nature, 1, 11, 25, 32, 55, 80, 88, 93
navigation, 33
necessity, 73, 87
need, 3, 8, 13, 14, 19, 21, 32, 34, 46, 48, 58, 61, 67, 80, 93
negativity, 2, 28
network, 7, 12, 24, 74, 85, 89, 98
networking, 13, 79
newfound, 14, 85
news, 75
non, 6, 8, 30, 58
norm, 1
notion, 11, 39
novel, 45
nuance, 33
Nyla, 1–19, 21–38, 41–44, 46–52, 55–89, 91, 92, 95–100
Nyla Ashen, 1, 2, 5, 7, 9, 23, 25–28, 32, 33, 42–44, 46–48, 57, 59, 60, 62, 64, 65, 67–70, 76, 79, 80, 82, 83, 85, 86, 88, 89, 95, 97–100

Nyla Ashen's, 2–5, 9, 11, 15, 17, 19, 21, 23, 26, 30, 31, 33–36, 41, 43, 48, 51, 52, 55, 57, 60, 64–66, 68, 69, 71, 72, 74, 76, 78, 82, 84, 87, 91, 92
Nyla comfort, 79
Nyla, 84

offer, 87, 89
office, 98
on, 1–7, 9–15, 17, 19, 21, 23, 24, 26, 30–38, 40, 41, 43–52, 55, 56, 58, 59, 61–70, 72–88, 91–95, 97–100
one, 2, 3, 7, 17, 26, 29, 30, 35, 38, 39, 46, 49, 50, 57, 64, 66, 68, 76–78, 81, 84, 86, 87, 97, 99, 100
opening, 45, 49, 50
openness, 76, 100
opinion, 41, 44, 58, 69, 92
opportunity, 12, 28, 33, 67, 83
opposition, 4, 8, 10, 22–25, 27, 77, 78, 80, 96, 99
oppression, 3, 73, 93
optimism, 50
order, 8, 11, 88, 89
organization, 12
organizing, 16, 43, 63–66, 73
orientation, 7, 13, 24, 28, 40, 45, 47, 51, 56, 59, 60, 65, 66, 79, 93, 95
other, 1, 7, 12, 18, 25, 30, 42, 47, 49, 57, 62, 65, 66, 73, 74, 80, 82, 89, 92, 93
outlet, 24
outpouring, 79
outreach, 13

pain, 6
painting, 89
Pakistan, 4
panel, 17, 18
parade, 83
parliament, 58
part, 14, 26, 35, 36, 83, 84
participation, 49
partner, 79, 83
partnership, 42, 44
passage, 30
passion, 6, 9, 12, 14, 17, 35, 55, 70, 72, 79, 80, 83, 92, 97, 99
path, 2, 3, 5, 7, 9, 10, 17, 60, 78, 82, 92, 93, 96
peace, 87
people, 8, 10, 16, 17, 21, 22, 27, 28, 31–34, 36, 38, 43, 48, 61, 65, 75, 77, 94
perception, 14, 24, 47
performance, 40, 74
persecution, 94
perseverance, 50, 67, 68
person, 38, 65, 72, 86, 97
personality, 3, 10
perspective, 3, 13, 14, 33, 87, 89
photography, 40
place, 2, 18, 31
plan, 23
platform, 4, 11, 12, 15, 18, 24, 28–32, 34, 40, 41, 43, 44, 58, 63, 72, 75, 76, 78, 85, 91, 98
play, 5, 12, 23, 41, 48, 62, 93
poem, 23
poetry, 74
point, 88
poise, 35
policy, 15, 22, 23, 40, 61, 64, 97, 98

pool, 18
population, 92, 94
portrayal, 45
position, 41
positivity, 78
potential, 8, 31, 39, 79, 83
power, 4–8, 10, 14, 16, 18, 22, 23, 25–28, 30–33, 35–41, 44–46, 48, 55, 60, 63–67, 71, 72, 74, 77, 78, 81–83, 87, 89, 95–98, 100
practice, 87
precedent, 30, 66, 74
prejudice, 1, 5, 7, 9, 21, 22, 33, 48, 51, 72, 84, 92, 93
presence, 4, 31, 34, 35, 37, 51, 72, 75, 76, 78, 99
pressure, 15, 24, 59, 79, 82, 87, 94
pride, 25, 40, 75, 83, 85
print, 22
priority, 11
privacy, 15
privilege, 26, 73
process, 39, 40, 60, 79, 80, 84–86, 88, 100
production, 39
professional, 4, 15, 84
profile, 44
progress, 4, 31, 55, 57, 59, 67, 73, 93–97, 99, 100
progression, 9
prominence, 10
promise, 97
protection, 56
public, 10–13, 15, 18, 19, 21, 22, 24, 30–32, 34, 38, 40, 41, 43, 44, 46–48, 55, 58, 65, 66, 69, 78, 82, 83, 92
purpose, 14, 15, 89

pursuit, 2, 4, 8, 56, 74, 90

Qirona, 23, 55, 56, 64, 65, 67, 72, 95
Qironan, 59
Qironans, 91
quest, 3, 44, 98
question, 2, 8, 9, 17, 34, 47, 50, 59
quo, 1, 10, 77

race, 73, 93
racism, 93
radio, 33
rainbow, 23
raising, 21–23, 41, 58, 66, 94
rally, 77
range, 4, 32, 36, 38, 44, 79
reach, 18, 26, 29, 31, 33, 41–43, 59, 75, 96, 97, 99
reality, 81
realization, 2, 3, 37
realm, 3, 63
recipient, 68, 70, 71
recognition, 18, 22, 56, 67–72, 91, 99
recourse, 7
reflection, 37, 49, 87
reform, 58
refusal, 7
rejection, 79, 84
relatability, 36, 49
relationship, 1, 5, 83
release, 24
reminder, 4, 11, 38, 48, 64, 78–81, 86, 87, 92
repeal, 59, 74, 91
representation, 10, 23, 32, 33, 36, 38–41, 44–46, 48, 76, 86, 92, 99
reputation, 10, 15

research, 3, 49, 50, 66, 73
resilience, 2, 4–11, 15, 18, 23, 25, 30, 35, 37, 43, 48, 50–52, 63, 71, 74–85, 87, 88, 92, 98–100
resistance, 24, 83, 87, 92
resolve, 6, 7, 14
resource, 5, 30
respect, 18, 27, 30, 33, 48, 57, 61, 86, 93, 97
respite, 80
response, 24, 33, 47, 49
responsibility, 1, 50
restroom, 30
result, 66
revision, 56
ridicule, 6
right, 56, 66, 67, 83, 84
rise, 6, 10, 77
road, 3
roadmap, 5
role, 2–6, 9, 12, 19, 26, 27, 29, 31, 33, 38, 39, 41, 43, 45, 46, 48, 56, 59, 61, 62, 68, 69, 75, 77, 78, 81, 83, 87, 91–95
routine, 80
ruling, 67
Ryan, 43
Ryan Hartley, 43

sacrifice, 11
safety, 83
Sarah, 4
Sarah Anderson, 4
sarcasm, 25, 28
satire, 8, 19, 25, 28, 36
scale, 33, 68, 69, 74, 75, 97
schedule, 88

school, 2, 23, 30, 61, 62, 75
screen, 38, 45
scrutiny, 10, 15, 46, 48, 82
section, 3, 4, 15, 21, 23, 26, 28, 31, 36, 38, 44, 46, 48, 55, 60, 66, 68, 69, 74, 76, 78, 82, 84, 86–88, 93, 95, 99
segment, 32
self, 2, 3, 6–9, 11, 12, 14–16, 24, 27, 28, 34, 36, 38, 43, 45, 47, 49, 50, 56, 72, 76–78, 80–89, 98, 100
sensation, 81
sense, 4, 8–12, 14–16, 24–26, 28, 32, 33, 36, 37, 40, 41, 44, 45, 49, 50, 62, 73, 76, 81, 88, 97
series, 18, 36, 44, 45, 87
seriousness, 29
serve, 31, 37, 38, 40, 48, 49, 69, 80, 81, 87, 100
set, 1, 10, 11, 56, 65, 66, 99, 100
sex, 22, 34, 56, 67, 74, 82, 94
sexism, 93
sexuality, 9, 11, 43, 47
shame, 86
shape, 13, 31, 44, 46, 52, 76, 78, 83, 98
share, 1, 14, 16, 18, 49, 63, 65, 72, 77, 79, 81, 85, 86, 94, 96
shift, 22, 66
show, 2, 6, 31, 32, 35, 45
side, 6, 79
sight, 29, 48
sign, 86, 89
significance, 10, 26, 38, 46, 58, 75, 89, 99
situation, 28, 83
size, 76

skill, 73
society, 3–6, 8, 9, 13, 15, 18, 19, 21–26, 31, 33–35, 38, 39, 47, 49, 51, 57–62, 64–66, 68, 70, 74, 75, 77, 82, 83, 91–97
socio, 93
solace, 1, 3, 4, 6, 7, 9, 12, 24, 80
solidarity, 10, 14, 32, 36, 42, 73
source, 4, 31, 48, 80, 83
space, 5, 9, 17, 19, 43, 80, 83–85
spark, 8, 16
speaker, 11, 49, 72
speaking, 10, 34, 66, 78, 88
special, 95
spectacle, 47
spectrum, 3
speculation, 46, 82
speech, 24, 31, 49, 50, 81
sphere, 7
spirit, 6–9, 70, 71, 78, 99, 100
spotlight, 10, 15, 44
sprint, 80
staff, 62
stage, 91
stance, 55, 91
statement, 29, 51
status, 1, 10, 68, 69, 77, 93
step, 57, 91, 95
stigma, 24
stigmatization, 94
stone, 92
Stonewall, 68
story, 2, 6, 7, 23, 45, 60, 77, 80, 83, 84, 86
storytelling, 8, 10, 13, 16, 21, 22, 25, 31, 32, 37, 40, 45, 46, 49, 51, 63–66, 72, 74, 98
strain, 80

stranger, 32
strategy, 8, 25, 27, 93
street, 16, 25
strength, 2–4, 6–10, 12, 14–16, 32, 43, 47, 48, 50, 79, 80, 84
stress, 87
struggle, 2, 33, 50, 79, 81, 89, 95
student, 62
style, 10, 19, 29
subject, 46
success, 73, 81
support, 2–8, 12–14, 17, 18, 22–24, 26, 27, 31, 32, 34, 37, 40, 43, 46, 47, 49, 50, 59, 62–65, 70, 75–77, 79–89, 94
supporter, 43
surprise, 10
surrounding, 7, 17, 19, 27, 29, 34, 36, 45–48, 59, 81, 86, 89, 98, 99
sustainability, 17
symbol, 51, 75, 76, 78, 100
system, 12, 55, 56, 58, 61, 62, 64–66, 81, 83, 91, 98, 99

tale, 9
talent, 36
talk, 10, 31–35, 49, 51, 75, 81
tapestry, 96
task, 18
Taylor Ford, 44
team, 22, 56, 66, 67, 88
technology, 63, 89
television, 22, 34, 35, 45, 92
tenacity, 56, 57, 98
termination, 67
terminology, 62

testament, 7, 43, 47, 69, 74, 77, 78, 82, 99, 100
text, 87
theater, 13, 40
therapy, 84, 86, 88, 94
thinking, 13, 28, 33, 64
thought, 13, 16, 25, 48, 49, 74, 75
threat, 79
time, 12, 14, 18, 37, 80, 81, 84–88
timing, 35
title, 70, 71
today, 1, 2, 93
toll, 11, 24, 79, 80, 83, 86
tongue, 28, 33
tool, 17, 27, 28, 30, 35, 40, 43, 47, 58, 86, 94, 99
topic, 29, 86
torch, 35, 97
town, 1, 5, 9
trademark, 76
trailblazer, 5, 9, 31, 68, 78
train, 71
training, 19, 56, 62, 64, 69, 94
trajectory, 15
transformation, 6, 9
transgender, 4, 30, 42, 43, 45, 56, 66, 67, 76
transphobia, 38, 62, 94
treatment, 34, 67
trepidation, 79
trick, 89
triumph, 6, 18, 44, 81
trust, 18
truth, 4, 10, 26, 47, 79
turn, 12, 33

uncertainty, 79
understanding, 2, 3, 7, 8, 13, 17–19, 21, 22, 25, 27, 28, 32–40, 43–49, 51, 55, 57, 59, 61–65, 72, 75, 77, 82–86, 89, 91–99
uniqueness, 1, 2, 49, 78
unity, 10, 16, 18, 26, 32, 33, 44, 50, 76, 96
up, 1, 2, 5, 6, 9, 19, 35, 39, 45, 49, 50, 60, 67, 76–78, 92, 95, 98, 99
upbringing, 1–5, 9, 84
urgency, 24
use, 4, 17, 29, 30, 38, 40, 44, 49, 71, 73

validation, 3, 38
value, 1, 16
variety, 39
victory, 66, 67
video, 36, 89
violation, 67
violence, 94
visibility, 23, 26, 33, 38, 40, 44–46, 52, 76, 84, 92, 99
vision, 7, 10, 25, 31, 41
voice, 7, 8, 10, 26, 44, 57, 60, 91
vulnerability, 16, 36, 79–82, 85

way, 8, 17, 19, 23, 25, 28, 34, 35, 46, 49, 55, 56, 59, 63–67, 71, 72, 74, 83, 89, 91, 98, 100
weakness, 86, 89
weight, 79, 80
well, 8, 11, 12, 15, 18, 24, 28, 33, 34, 38, 48, 66, 69, 70, 76, 80, 81, 86–90, 94, 95, 98, 100
willingness, 5, 16, 27
wisdom, 82, 95
wit, 8, 10, 13, 19, 25, 28, 29, 33, 35, 36, 71, 76, 92, 99

woman, 1, 58, 66
word, 74
wordplay, 19, 28
work, 5, 14, 16, 40, 47, 48, 51, 57, 60, 63, 64, 68–70, 73, 77, 80, 81, 85, 87, 89, 92, 93, 99
workload, 89
workplace, 23, 56, 66, 67
world, 2–4, 6, 7, 9–11, 14, 19, 23, 29, 35, 37, 40, 41, 43, 46, 50–52, 60, 69, 70, 72–78, 81, 89, 94, 95, 97–100
worth, 5, 15, 57, 96
writing, 39, 98

yoga, 87, 88
youth, 11, 12, 17, 21, 22, 30, 35, 39, 43, 51, 52, 66, 69, 71, 75, 78, 88, 98, 99

Zara, 4
Zara Ahmed, 4

Milton Keynes UK
Ingram Content Group UK Ltd.
UKHW020319021124
450424UK00013B/1338